What people are saying about
Grandparenting with a

"Lillian Penner has written an excellent book on prayer that I wish I could get into the hands of every grandparent. You should purchase this book for four reasons:

- You will be trained to keep Scripture central to your prayers;
- Lillian equips you to be an intentional grandparent who focuses on the spiritual growth of grandchildren;
- You will find many practical tools to help you develop the habit of praying for grandchildren;
- Lillian rightly understands something that Oswald Chambers once said, 'Prayer doesn't equip us for greater work prayer is the greater work.' When grandparents ask me for a book on prayer, I always recommend Lillian's book, and I highly recommend it to you."

Josh Mulvihill, PhD, Executive Director of Church and Family Ministry at Renewanation, and has served as a pastor for nearly twenty years.

"There is a spiritual renaissance brewing in North America, and at the core of this renewal are praying grandparents. As is the case in every major awakening in past centuries, humble and passionate prayer is a catalyst which spiritually connects generations. That's why I highly recommend Lillian Penner's book, *Grandparenting with a Purpose: Effective Ways to Pray for Your Grandchildren*. It is a straightforward and practical guide to remind us all to pray. It has inspired me. For any grandparent who hungers for supernatural strength and insight and who labors on behalf of their children and grandchildren, this book is a must read."

Ken R. Canfield, PhD., Founder, National Association for Grandparenting and Grands Matter!

"We were encouraged with the many ideas the author gives grandparents on how to connect with their grandchildren, encourage them, and pray for them. She obviously has a lot of experience in praying for her own and a great heart after God's heart. We hope this book encourages you as it encouraged us to get connected with and to pray more specifically and regularly for your grandchildren!"

Lee Talley, Calvary Chapel pastor in Willows, CA

"I love this book! Within one month I saw immediate and positive responses from my four grandsons. One of the author's suggestions is that we tell our grandchildren we are praying for them and ask them specifically what they would like us to pray for. They were all surprised to find out that I pray for them on a specific day of the week, and I was surprised when each one of them told me something they wanted me to pray for. This is a great book to help you pray for your grandchildren. It not only gave me biblical guidance on prayer, but it also gave me great suggestions, ideas, and tools to help me pray more deliberately for each one. It doesn't matter what ages your grandchildren are, this book will help you in your prayer life. What better glory can we bring to God than to pray for the generations to come?"

Caroline Miller, a Grandmother in Oregon

"Praying consistently and persistently for our grandchildren is the greatest gift we can give them, no matter whether they live near us or halfway around the world. This book will help you pray with more passion and purpose as you lift those precious grandchildren and their needs to the Lord each day. It is our privilege to pray biblical and practical prayers for them, as we trust God to work in their lives. May each of us leave a lasting legacy to our children's children, one that will continue for generations to come—a legacy of spiritual influence and prayer. Grandparents, let us pray right now. For starters, Bible verses in this book will help guide you in your prayer life."

Quin Sherrer, co-author of *Grandma, I Need Your Prayers*

"For any age or stage of the grandchildren in your life, grab bunches of ideas from Lillian Penner. Bursting with creativity and practical applications, these pages of Christ-honoring wisdom will equip you to cultivate godliness with this generation."

Peggy Powell, producer of "Praying Grandmothers" Newsletter

Revised & Expanded

GRANDPARENTING
with a Purpose

Effective Ways to Pray for your Grandchildren

REVISED & EXPANDED

GRANDPARENTING
with a Purpose

Effective Ways to Pray for your Grandchildren

Lillian Penner

REDEMPTION PRESS

Published by Redemption Press, PO Box 427, Enumclaw, WA 98022.

Toll Free (844) 2REDEEM (273-3336)

Redemption Press is honored to present this title in partnership with the author. The views expressed or implied in this work are those of the author. Redemption Press provides our imprint seal representing design excellence, creative content and high quality production.

Unless otherwise noted, all Scripture quotations in this book are taken from the Holy Bible, New International Version®. NIV®. Copyright © 1973, 1978, 1984 by International Bible Society. Used by permission of Zondervan. All rights reserved.

Scriptural quotations marked (NLT) are taken from the Holy Bible, New Living Translation, copyright © 2008. Used by permission of Tyndale House Publishers, Inc., Wheaton, IL 60189 USA. All rights reserved.

Scriptural quotations marked (TLB) are taken from The Living Bible, copyright © 1971. Used by permission of Tyndale House Publishers, Inc., Wheaton, IL 60189 USA. All rights reserved.

Because of the dynamic nature of the Internet, any Web addresses or links contained in this book may have changed since publication and may no longer be valid.

ISBN 13: 978-1-63232-573-0 (Print)
       978-1-63232-584-6 (ePub)
       978-1-63232-585-3 (Mobi)

Library of Congress Control Number: 2010939422

Dedication

To my paternal and maternal great-grandparents, my grandparents, and my parents, who have, by their examples and prayers, passed on their godly legacy to me, my three married sons, my nine grandchildren, five great-grandchildren, and my future generations.

"The memory of the righteous will be a blessing."
(Proverbs 10:7)

Acknowledgments

I greatly appreciate the legacy passed on by my family as they modeled their walk with the Lord and invested their prayers in my life. In response, God gave me a passion of praying for my grandchildren and for sharing this passion with other grandparents, so they, too, can share the joy and rewards of intercessory prayer for their grandchildren.

I want to thank God for the incredible things he has done in my life as he directed my path in the struggle to write this book, as the enemy opposed the contents.

I thank God for the many friends he provided to walk the journey with me and for their encouragement, prayers, and invaluable help with the manuscript. I would like to thank Sherry Schumann, Cathy Jacobs, and Ken Canfield for their encouragement throughout the process.

I want to thank all those who shared their prayers and their stories of how their grandparents' prayers affected their lives.

I want to thank my faithful prayer partners who prayed to make this book a reality. Most of all, I want to thank my dear husband, John, for listening to me, for sharing his ideas, support, editing, and being there for me in the process.

Foreword

Some of my earliest memories are of my grandparents kneeling in their home to pray for the lost and their own families. My grandparents took prayer seriously. I am convinced their prayers, combined with their authentic Christlike examples, played a key role in my desire, and that of my five siblings and numerous cousins, to follow Christ.

Perhaps at no other time in our history has a call to prayer been as critical for the body of Christ as it is today. Lillian Penner understands this urgency of our day. She wrote this book to call each of us to our knees. She is serious about the power of prayer to keep the hearts and minds of our grandchildren from falling captive to the enemy's deception and lies. We are engaged in a spiritual battle that requires spiritual weapons. Prayer is the command center for our warfare.

What you hold in your hand is a tool Lillian has provided for engaging in this war on behalf of your children and grandchildren. It is not another wimpy plea to say a prayer from time to time for your grandchildren and family. This is a challenge, not for the faint-hearted, but for passionate, intentional grandmothers and grandfathers who are willing to get on their knees daily to intercede and plead for their grandchildren's salvation and protection from the Evil One. It requires courageous and persistent action by grandparents who will not only pray, but will authentically represent Christ and His gospel by example for the next generations. This is not about feel-good, comfortable prayers we utter when it is convenient, but the continual, fervent prayers of righteous saints whose faith is real, engaged, and steadfast. Lillian has written something that God can use to change lives, including your own, and it is worthy of more than a cursory read. This is a dangerous book because once you read it there will be no doubt about what you must do. If you truly believe God and His Word, if you are committed to making Christ preeminent in all your life, and if you are willing to embrace the Father's heart for the "little ones," then by all means, read on.

Since you are still reading, I hope that means you are ready to count the cost and offer yourself as a conduit for God's blessing, salvation, and power to be poured out through you for your grandchildren. There is no doubt it will be a challenging and difficult task, but remember God has promised a great reward for those who believe He exists and He rewards those who earnestly seek Him. Seek Him now with all your heart for the sake of your children. This is a journey worth taking. Your children, grandchildren, and their children will call you blessed.

Cavin T. Harper
Executive Director
Christian Grandparenting Network

Contents

Section III: Standing in the Gap for the Grandchildren

Appendix...157

Invitation to Stand in the Gap

God has given most of us the special gift of grandparent-ing when we approach our midlife season. The privilege of being a grandparent frequently is called "the frosting on the cake." It's a very special time in life.

We are living in challenging times as the world is sinking into spiritual depravity. The media-driven cul-ture is desensitizing our grandchildren, and many of our grandchildren's role models are disappointing them.

However, God has given us a sacred trust, an opportu-nity to imprint a child's life with God's faithfulness. Just as Esther stood in the gap for her people, the Israel-ites, when their lives were threatened, we can stand in the gap for our grandchildren with our examples and our prayers. By reflecting our love for God, we share how He has blessed us as we have walked with him and are continuing to grow in our relationship with him.

A few years ago on a sunny autumn day, my husband and I were traveling in the beautiful Rocky Mountains of Colorado. Frequently, we saw the rugged snow-cov-ered mountains and golden aspen trees reflecting in a lake. As I was pondering the awesome sight, I could not help but ask myself: *Does God's love reflect from my life to my children and grandchildren like the mountains reflect on the lake? Do they see Jesus in me?* Considering these questions and the possible answers led me to realize that the sun needs to shine on the water for there to be a reflection. In order for God's love to reflect from my life, the love of God's Son, Jesus Christ, must shine in my heart.

Since our world is in moral and spiritual decline, we are in a battle for the minds and hearts of our dear grandchildren. The enemy is trying to steal their lives and the plans God has for them. In addition to trying to destroy their faith, the enemy is trying to destroy the morals of our country, especially the family unit. It is urgent that we stand in the gap to pray for the spiritual, emotional, and physical protection of our grandchildren and their parents so they do not become victims of our culture.

I invite you to use the resources in this book to help you stand in the gap to pray intentionally and deliberately, reflecting the face of God to your grandchildren. I hope and pray this book will challenge you to be your grandchildren's prayer warrior and ask Jesus Christ to do great works in their lives.

Blessings,
Lillian Penner

> "The earnest prayer of a righteous person has great power and produces wonderful results"
> (James 5:16, NLT).

Section I

Grandparents Standing in the Gap with Prayer

"I looked for someone who might rebuild the wall
of righteousness that guards the land. I searched
for someone to stand in the gap in the wall so I
wouldn't have to destroy the land, but I found no one"
(Ezekiel 22:30 NLT).

Do you believe God has a design for grandparents?

It is God's design for grandparents to pass their faith to multiple generations. Just as David was chosen for his generation, God has positioned us, as grandparents, for this generation with our personality and gifts for our families. We read in Acts 16:36 "David served God's purpose in his generation."

Today's design for grandparents

Moses told the Israelites, "Only be careful, and watch yourselves closely so that you do not forget the things your eyes have seen or let them fade from your heart as long as you live. Teach them to your children and their children after them" (Deuteronomy 4:9). Today grandparents have the same design for their grandparenting roles.

Asaph also gives us directions in Psalm 78:1-8 NLT):

"O my people, listen to my instructions. Open your ears to what I am saying, for I will speak to you in a parable. I will teach you hidden lessons from our past stories we have heard and known, stories our ancestors handed down to us. We will not hide these truths from our children; we will tell the next generation about the glorious deeds of the Lord, about his power and his mighty wonders. For he issued his laws to Jacob; he gave his instructions to Israel. He commanded our ancestors to teach them to their children so the next generation might know them—even the children not yet born—and they in turn will teach their own children. So each generation should set its hope anew on God, not forgetting his glorious miracles and obeying his commands. Then they will not be like their ancestors—stubborn, rebellious, and unfaithful, refusing to give their hearts to God."(NLT)

God's design for grandparenting is twofold: to teach HOPE in God and OBEDIENCE.

Our walk must match our talk

Our grandchildren are watching and listening to see if our life choices match our stated convictions. How we live our lives is a powerful example to our families. The best gifts we can give our families are not expensive luxuries but a good name. According to Proverbs 22:1, "A good name is better than wealth." If we nurture our relationships with our children and grandchildren, we will speak into their lives and help shape their hearts.

Can grandparents make a difference?

Grandparents can make a difference. Grandparents can help their grandchildren navigate the rapid cultural shifts we are experiencing. The enemy is undermining God's design for our grandchildren by filling our headlines and social media feeds with a world view. However, God has begun a powerful movement to awaken Christian grandparents to make a spiritual impact for the next generation.

God chose us for our specific children, grandchildren, and great-grandchildren. We are not living in past generations or future generations. We are living in this present generation, with God's purpose. He gave us an instruction book, God's Word, to follow.

My husband and I were chosen for this generation for our three sons, three daughters-in-law, nine grandchildren, their spouses, and four great-granddaughters—to love, cherish, pray for, and encourage them to follow Jesus. **He has chosen you for your family.**

Study Guide
For personal reflection or group discussion

1. Ask God, how do you want me to fulfill your purpose for my generation?
2. Are my grandchildren watching my walk with the Lord?
3. Is my walk with the Lord what I want my grandchildren to follow?
4. How am I teaching my grandchildren to live in obedience to God's Word?
5. Will my grandchildren want my Jesus?

"Follow my example, as I follow the example of Christ"
(1 Corinthians 11:1).

"In everything set an example by doing what is good."
(Titus 2:7)

God Uses People to Bridge the Gap

The Bible describes prayer as "standing in the gap" or "bridging the gap," the channel through which God's will is brought to earth. We are going to look in God's Word to see some examples of people he used to stand in the gap so his purpose could be accomplished.

God appointed Moses to stand in the gap between his people, the Israelites, and Pharaoh. Esther stood in the gap for her people, the Israelites, with prayer and fasting when Haman wanted to destroy them.

God was grieved and his heart was filled with pain because the earth was corrupt and filled with violence. But God used Noah, a man with whom he found favor, a righteous man, blameless among the people of his time, and Noah walked with God. So God chose Noah, his wife, their three sons and their wives to stand in the gap, safe in the ark while God flooded the earth, and all other living creatures perished.

After God created the earth, he said, "It was very good" (Genesis 1:31). There was no gap between God and the earth. However, after Adam and Eve sinned, sin created a gap between God and what he had planned for the earth.

Fortunately, God stood in the gap for us by sending his Son, Jesus, to the earth to live as a man, die for our sins, and arise from the dead so we could have a personal relationship with him.

God is our source of power, and he chose us to be intercessors, a channel for his power to bridge the gap between himself and the earth. Daniel knew that prayer was the means that would bring God's will from heaven, cause his will to be activated, and release his power for his purpose on earth.

God chose us, as grandparents, to partner with him on behalf of our children, grandchildren, and future generations to share in his work and blessings. Jennifer Kennedy Dean writes in her Bible study, Live a Praying Life, "Prayer is the most aggressive, offensive, proactive, invasive work you can ever engage in."[1]

Just as Jesus, Moses, Esther, Daniel, Noah, and many others in the Bible stood in the gap, grandparents have the privilege to stand in the gap with prayer for our families. Satan is very active in the world today; he knows his time is short. It is time for grandparents to urgently and intentionally pray for God's physical, emotional, and spiritual protection for our family members.

Paul writes in Ephesians 6:10-18 that we are to be strong and firm in our relationship with the Lord. We are to stand firm against Satan's well-thought-out plans for our children, our grandchildren, and ourselves. In order to recognize the deception of the world, we, along with our grandchildren and their parents, must know the truth.

Since we are living in a time where truth is challenged in the classrooms, it is not only essential to pray for our families individually, but for grandparents to unite in prayer for our families. As Co-Prayer Director for Christian Grandparenting Network, I would like to encourage you to join other grandparents praying for their families.

Most Grandparents@Prayer intercessory prayer groups meet once a month for about an hour and half to get acquainted with one another and pray for their grandchildren. It's a safe place for grandparents to share their concerns and rest in the knowledge that others are praying with you.

As grandparents, we can make a difference in the world by praying regularly and deliberately for our grandchildren and their parents. It is our responsibility to powerfully touch the lives of their generation, for eternity, through prayer.

You will find more Grandparents@Prayer information and testimonials in the Appendix of this book.

As grandparents, let us be the channels through which God's will is brought down to earth for our children, grandchildren, future generations, and ourselves.

Study Guide
For personal reflection or group discussion

- Can you think of any other Bible character(s) who stood in the gap for their people?
- How can we bridge the gap for our grandchildren?
- How do you see the enemy distracting your grandchildren and their parents?
- What can we do for our grandchildren to help them know the truth?
- As grandparents, what is our spiritual responsibility to reach the next generation for eternity?

Prayer
Dear Father, show me where and how you want me to stand in the gap with prayer for my grandchildren and their parents. In Jesus' name, amen.

Reflecting on My Journey of Praying for My Grandchildren

God blessed my husband and me with nine grandchildren ranging in age from sixteen to thirty-seven years of age. For many years, I felt my prayers for them were too general because, as a long-distance grandmother, I was often unaware of what was going on in their lives. I prayed that God would bless them, but, ultimately, I grew frustrated. Something was lacking in my vague, general prayers. I asked God to show me how to become intentional in praying for them.

Encouragement

My prayers for my grandchildren changed dramatically after I read *Grandma, I Need Your Prayers,* by Quin Sheerer & Ruthanne Garlock, and *When Mothers Pray,* by Cheri Fuller. Both are full of practical advice and encouraged me to use specific Scriptures in my prayers. As a result, God's Word became a manual, not only teaching me to pray more effectively, but also reminding me that prayer is connecting me to the creator of the universe. Praying God's Word enabled me to pray with more confidence and boldness. It also motivated me to pray regularly and specifically for the emotional, physical, and spiritual well-being of my grandchildren.

Primary Prayer

My primary prayer for my grandchildren is that they will come to realize God loves them, to accept Jesus Christ as their personal Savior, and to follow Christ wholeheartedly throughout their lives. God has created each of my grandchildren for a unique purpose. I pray that they will discover their purpose, be motivated to pursue it, and trust him to provide the resources to enable them to do so. Only God can provide fulfillment. The world cannot.

Holy Spirit Intercedes

I learned from Romans 8:26 that the Holy Spirit intercedes for me when I do not know exactly what or how to pray for someone, and my prayers took on new meaning. The Holy Spirit knows the needs of my grandchildren, so I ask him to intercede for me according to his will. It is comforting to know I can put my concerns in God's hands instead of carrying them myself.

Often, my prayers are not answered as I ask or on my timetable. However, in the waiting God does amazing things, both in my life and in the lives of my grandchildren.

Communication

New channels of communication opened with my older grandchildren when I started asking how I might pray for them. In the case of the young ones, I consulted with their parents to keep abreast of specific concerns. That enabled me to pray more specifically for them. Calling or sending greeting cards offers encouragement and remind them that I love and pray for them. The electronic age offers new opportunities to stay in touch with e-cards, e-mail, and texts. The first time I texted my oldest granddaughter, she texted back a surprised, "WOW! You are incredible!" I continue to text my older grandchildren occasionally, just to let them know I'm thinking of them and praying for them.

It is important for me to communicate my love and acceptance, even though I may not agree with their life choices at times. My interest in the details of their lives along with my desire to pray over those details, speaks accepting love to their hearts.

Photo Prayer Journal

In her book, *When Mother's Pray,* Cheri Fuller suggests making a photo prayer journal for your grandchildren. The photo prayer journal is a working document to help you pray intentionally and effectively for your grandchildren. I developed a photo prayer journal in a three-ring binder, which features a section for each grandchild. Each section includes a profile sheet with the grandchild's photograph, other personal information, and pages on which to write prayer concerns, hopes, and dreams for that grandchild. (See the Appendix for more on the photo prayer journal.)

Blessings as a Result

A note from my oldest granddaughter confirms that praying for our precious grandchildren is never a wasted effort: "Your phone calls, cards, and e-mails were encouraging and made a significant impact on my life, especially in my teenage and college years. Your prayers and encouragement have been rock-solid reminders of God's truth in my incredible, crazy life-shaping years, and now in my married life. Your prayers help me surrender the craziness of my life to God."

Using a photo prayer journal in my prayer time has strengthened my relationships with my grandchildren. Whether they live nearby or far away, praying for them intentionally keeps me in touch. When I let them know I am praying for them, my prayers can often be as powerful as my presence, especially when they are older and busy with school and work.

As a grandparent, I can have a major role in stabilizing and influencing the lives of my grandchildren, both through my personal example and through my prayers for them during these turbulent years. Praying intentionally for my grandchildren has given me purpose and fulfillment. I believe that the seeds of prayer I plant today will yield a harvest of blessing for them in the future.

Study Guide
For personal reflection or group discussion

- How would you rate your prayer life for your grandchildren? (1-10)
- What has inspired you to pray intentionally for your children and grandchildren?
- Do you speak Scripture when you pray?
- What is your primary prayer for your grandchildren?
- Do you know what to pray for your grandchildren?
- How can the Holy Spirit help you to pray for your grandchildren when you don't know how to pray for them?

"No eye has seen, no ear has heard, no mind has conceived
what God has prepared for those who love him"
(1 Corinthians 2:9).

Grandparents Reflect Christ by Example

By the time they come to the autumn season of their lives, grandparents have encountered and survived many life challenges. This is the time to share how we have dealt with life's challenges in the past and how we are dealing with them now so that we can make a significant impact on our grandchildren.

My Grandmother's Example

When I was a young woman, I attended college in the town where my lonely, widowed grandmother lived. I had many opportunities to visit her. As she grieved my grandfather's death, she demonstrated her trust in God to care for her and showed how God sustained her each day by claiming the promise Jesus gave his disciples after his resurrection. "And be sure of this, I am with you always" (Matthew 28:20).

My grandmother's faith that God would always be there for her made a great impact on my life. Her testimony influenced me to incorporate that verse in the daily experiences of my life. Since those early adult years, whenever life has been difficult, disappointing, or downright discouraging, I have claimed that same Scripture verse. My prayer is that I, too, will have opportunities to share my life experiences of trusting God with my children and grandchildren.

Reflecting Christ by Example

Paul wrote to Titus, "You yourself must be an example to them by doing good deeds of every kind. Let everything you do reflect the integrity and seriousness of your teaching" (Titus 2:7 NLT). Titus was to set an example by doing good works of every kind and by showing integrity, sincerity, and honesty. *Integrity* is adhering to a code of values being trustworthy and genuine. *Sincerity* is honesty, genuineness, and authenticity. Paul instructed Titus to model a life of integrity, sincerity, and genuineness. We, too, should be teaching our grandchildren by example to do good deeds of every kind, not because they are trying to earn praise, but because they love God and want to demonstrate his love to others.

A Powerful Tool

God has given us a powerful tool with which to influence our grandchildren—the way we live our own lives. As spiritual role models, we can demonstrate the reality of our faith by walking with God through both the storms and sunny days of our lives. God has given grandparents the responsibility to set a positive example. We *do* affect our grandchildren one way or another. Will it be positively or negatively?

On the way to a restaurant one day, my then twelve-year-old grandchild said we should say she was only eleven so she could eat for the children's price. While the motivation might have been to save me money, the event provided an opportunity to set a good example. We chose to tell the truth and pay the extra money. Later, we were able to discuss the importance of integrity, even in supposedly "little things."

Grandparent's Role

The role of godly grandparents is to communicate their faith in Jesus Christ, praying specifically and diligently for their grandchildren. We are also to tell future generations how God has walked with us and demonstrated his mighty works in our lives. Some of our greatest blessings will come after we ask God to use us to touch our grandchildren's lives and we get to see the results. If you are overwhelmed with how to be a good influence on your grandchildren, God is waiting for you to ask for wisdom. Look for opportunities to talk about what God has done for you.

In Proverbs 27:19 we read, "As a face is reflected in water, so the heart reflects the real person" (NLT). What does the reflection of our "real person" look like? When we are committed to read and meditate on God's Word, we reflect a life transformed into his image. We glorify God when we reveal or manifest his character by the way we live, demonstrating God's love to those around us.

The Reflection of a Godly Woman's Faith

Recently, a dear cousin went to be with the Lord. She was a godly woman who loved the Lord, loved her family, and lived a long, full life. Her commitment to the Lord and her family were obvious in her concern and prayers for her children, grandchildren, and great-grandchildren. The road her family traveled had many rough spots, but she committed them to the Lord, and he walked with them.

Her family misses her. However, their memories of her love for God will continue to bear fruit in their lives in the years ahead. She has experienced the crown of blessings for the righteous. Her family has the blessing of remembering *a righteous woman who prayed for them.*

Grandparents who love the Lord have a responsibility to reproduce their faith. Our grandchildren will usually mirror our walk, whatever it is. My grandmother made a lasting impression on my life because she reflected her faith in God's provision to sustain her during her time of grieving for my grandfather. When we share God's love with our grandchildren, and, as a result, they walk with the Lord, our love for God will keep on living through our grandchildren, even after we are gone.

Prayer, the Greatest Gift

In the Bible, we read about many people God used in the autumn season of life for life's greatest work. According to God's Word, God wants us to focus on passing our spiritual legacy to the next generation. The material things we leave our grandchildren are temporary; however, our prayers and examples can make a significant impact on them for a lifetime. Prayer is the greatest gift we can give our grandchildren.

Do your grandchildren see an authenticity and sincerity about you in your relationship with God? What a blessing it would be for me to hear my grandchildren say, "I want to have a relationship with the Lord like my grandparents modeled for me."

I hope I can say in the years to come, "I have no greater joy than to hear that my children and grandchildren are walking in the truth" (3 John 1:4).

Ask yourself:

- What kind of memories will my children and grandchildren remember when I pass away?
- Is my walk with the Lord what I want reflected in the lives of my grandchildren?
- Do I want my grandchildren to imitate my spiritual life?
- Will they want my Jesus?
- Will my love for God keep on living through my grandchildren, even after I am deceased?

"The LORD hears the prayer of the righteous"
(Proverbs 15:29).

Study Guide
For personal reflection or group discussion

- Do you have a testimony from your grandparents?
- How are you teaching your grandchildren *integrity* and *sincerity*?
- Are you demonstrating a positive or negative example by the way you live your life?
- What is the role of a godly grandparent?
- How are you reflecting your faith to your grandchildren?
- Do your grandchildren see an authenticity and sincerity in your relationship with God?

Prayer

Lord, forgive me when I have not taken the time to be in your Word or modeled the life of a godly grandparent. Help me to take the time to read and meditate on your Word every day so I will reflect your face in the heart of my grandchildren. Help me to be a godly example and model good deeds, teaching my grandchildren to live lives of truth with integrity, authenticity, and seriousness. Help me to give sound, wise, wholesome counsel and guidance, encouraging my grandchildren to demonstrate God's love to others. In Jesus' name, amen.

The Ripple Effect of Praying Grandparents

During the summer, many grandparents will vacation with their grandchildren. Some will go camping. It is a great opportunity to spend extra time with the possibility of quality interaction. Now imagine you are camping with your grandchildren in the mountains. You have cooked your campfire stew for dinner and you are relaxing around the campfire beside a big lake. It is perfectly still; there is no wind. The lake is a mirror reflecting a beautiful sunset. Your grandchildren skip stones across the lake's glassy surface. They are enthralled with seeing who can make the biggest ripples.

Grandpa tells Grandma, "Just as the kids are making ripples in the water with the rocks, we can make ripples in the lives of our grandchildren with our prayers." Our prayers for our grandchildren to invite Jesus Christ into other lives and to walk with Him throughout their lives will have a ripple effect on their families and friends, their world, and their future.

Another way we as grandparents can have a ripple effect on the lives of our grandchildren is by the way we live our lives. As we seek the Lord, investing time, energy, and effort in our spiritual walk with Him, our examples will have a ripple effect on our children, grandchildren, and future generations.

My Great-Grandfather's Prayer

I found a letter in my family archives, written by my great-grandfather in Poland and addressed to my grandfather who had immigrated to America. In the letter, he wrote that he was praying for my grandfather and his future generations. It was a special blessing for me to see in writing that my great-grandfather prayed for me before I was born. His prayers had a ripple effect on my grandparents, my parents, my life, my children, and my grandchildren.

You can have the privilege of starting the ripples in your family, even if you do not have a Christian heritage. Prayer is the greatest gift we can give our family. Our families need material things, but those things are only temporary. Our prayers will affect them for many generations.

My Friend's Story

I would like to share the story my friend shared with me of how her grandparents influenced her life, even though her parents did not influence her spiritually. She said, "I grew up in a non-Christian home. My father's father was a minister, and his mother was a devoted Christian. My mother's parents were also church-going people. However, my parents rebelled against God and the church, even though they both grew up in Christian homes.

"My grandparents took their responsibility very seriously, and my spiritual influence was a high priority for them. I remember hearing my father's father pray for me when I was a young child visiting in their home. Although my father's parents died while I was a child, I respected them very much.

"My mother's parents often told me, 'We are praying for you.' As a young child, my neighbors invited me to go to church with them, and as a result, I asked

Jesus into my heart. My grandparents were thankful to know their prayers were answered before they passed away, even though my parents did not teach me about Jesus or take me to church. It means so much to me that both sets of my grandparents let me know they prayed for me. I strongly believe the prayers of my grandparents led me to invite Jesus Christ into my life, marry a Christian young man, and be actively involved in my church. I only remember my parents attending church with me one time, and that was many years after I was married. However, as a result of my praying grandparents, my children and my grandchildren have a personal relationship with Jesus Christ and carry on the faith."

Even though my friend's spiritually rebellious parents interrupted the ripple effect, the intentional prayers of her grandparents passed their heritage of faith to the future generations, and the ripples continued.

Be a Prayer Warrior

God has placed our grandchildren in our families so we can be their prayer warriors. He has given us the awesome opportunity to partner with Him on behalf of these dear ones. He has given me nine grandchildren to pray for, and He has given you your grandchildren.

Sometimes, as we get older and are limited physically, we might feel useless. However, if we have grandchildren, God has a purpose for keeping us on this earth—to be *prayer warriors* for our grandchildren who are living in this spiritually deprived world.

Study Guide
For personal reflection or group discussion

- How can you have a ripple effect on the lives of your grandchildren?
- Are you creating a ripple effect on your family?
- Are you praying for your future generations?
- Do you communicate to your children and grandchildren that you are praying for them?
- If so, how do you communicate that to them?
- Did your grandparents communicate to you that they were praying for you?

Communicate your Faith to Your Grandchildren

Grandparents love to boast about their grandchildren and are ready to show their pictures to anyone who will look at them. Grandmothers used to carry "brag books." However, in this electronic age, many grandparents store pictures of their grandchildren in their cell phones. The pictures are always conveniently accessible to show.

Joy Brings Responsibility

With the joy of grandchildren comes a responsibility. God has given each generation a responsibility to pass on its heritage of faith to children and future descendants. God has placed our grandchildren in our sphere of influence for such a time as this. What a privilege we have to co-partner with God to rescue them from the dangers of the world.

Our grandchildren are growing up in unstable, crucial times with much turmoil in our culture. Naturally, a father would want to rescue his child from danger, if the child were running into the street. Spiritually, Jesus rescued us and paid the price for our sins so we can have a personal relationship with him. We have a responsibility to pray for the rescue of our grandchildren.

Fight for Your Family

When Nehemiah faced opposition in rebuilding the wall in Jerusalem, he told the people, "Don't be afraid of them. Remember the Lord, who is great and awesome, and fight for your brothers, sons, and your daughters, your wives and your homes" (Nehemiah 4:14). Just as Nehemiah asked the people to fight for their families, we as grandparents need to use our prayers to fight the opposition that our children and grandchildren face each day.

Abraham Lincoln said, "A child is a person who is going to carry on what you have started. He is going to sit where you are sitting, and when you are gone, attend to those things which you think are important ... The fate of humanity is in his hands."[1] If you are like most Christian grandparents, you would like your grandchildren to place their faith in Jesus Christ. As the moral and spiritual climate in our world is eroding, it is becoming more difficult for our grandchildren to grow up in a Christlike environment.

Fighting the opposition with our prayers for the ongoing guidance and spiritual growth of our grandchildren takes daily discipline. To pray effectively, we need to know their frustrations, dreams, fears, concerns, and expectations. Now and then, we need to ask them, "What is going on in your life right now? How can I pray for you?" We also need to ask their parents how we can specifically pray for them.

To fight for our families as Nehemiah told the Israelites to do, we have to pray intentionally and regularly. According to God's Word, praying for our children and grandchildren should be a high priority. Not all prayers are going to be answered immediately or even in our lifetimes. However, God will acknowledge our intercessory prayers and answer them at just the right time.

Did Your Grandparents Pray for You?

I asked a number of my friends if their grandparents prayed for them. The response I received most often was, "Surely, they prayed for me; they were Christians and went to church." Then I asked, "Did your grandparents ever tell you they were praying for you?" Most of them said, "No, they never told me." My heart was broken to hear this. It is very important that the grandchildren know their grandparents are praying for them. Have you shared with your grandchildren you are praying for them? Grandparents are fond of giving gifts to their grandchildren, but the greatest gift we can pass on to them is the gift of a praying grandparent.

The most important task we have as grandparents is to communicate our faith in Christ. A family's faith can be lost in one generation; however, we as grandparents can be defenders of our faith. Life is full of disappointments and crises. If our children and grandchildren turn their backs on their heritage of faith, they will face these challenges and trials without God in a chaotic world.

Truths to Pass On

I learned some important truths in a Beth Moore Bible study, *Believing God* [2] that I would like to pass on to my children and grandchildren. They are:

- God is who he says he is.
- God can do what he says He can do.
- I am who God says I am.
- I can do all things through Christ who strengthens me.
- God's Word is alive and active in me.

When we, as grandparents, unite in prayer to pray for our grandchildren we threaten the enemy (Satan). Our children and grandchildren desperately need our prayers in this morally and spiritually deprived culture we live in. Communicate your faith.

A Praying Grandmother

My friend Barb shared with me how her ninety-seven-year-old grandmother reflected her life to her family with her prayers: "My grandmother prays for me by name as well as my husband, children, and grandson every day. She has prayed specifically for us and claimed God's promises, seeing many of her prayers answered. She has a heart for prayer and has prayed for each of her children, grandchildren, great-grandchildren, great-great-grandchildren, and her extended family members for as long as they can remember. Many of her grandchildren, great-grandchildren and great-great-grandchildren do not know her very well, as most of us do not live near her.

"However, we all know the precious legacy she is leaving and will continue to leave until God takes her home. I believe she has been the strength of our family and the example of God's love as a Shepherd who will not rest until each sheep has returned to the flock. Perhaps that is why she is still with us, her prayers are leading the last sheep home."

God sees our grandchildren as individuals, so we need to pray for them by name individually. Are you praying for your grandchildren by name, or do you group them all together? There may be times when we group them together, but it is important that we also pray for them all individually. According to Revelation 21:27, God writes each of our names in the Lamb's Book of Life when we accept him as our personal Savior.

God has placed each of our children, grandchildren, and great-grandchildren in our lives to uphold in prayer. Have you thought about how many people are praying for your grandchildren?

Spiritual Trust Find

We may not have wealth to pass on to our children, grandchildren, and future descendants. However, author Jennifer Kennedy Dean shares in her book, *The Legacy of Prayer*, about a spiritual trust fund that will only increase in value. She writes, "We can leave behind for our descendants a spiritual trust that can never be stolen, squandered, or lost. We can lay up a storehouse of imperishable wealth by praying for our grandchildren and future generations. Our prayers are deposits in their spiritual trust fund and will be for withdrawals when needed."[3]

I believe that truth also pertains to our prayers when we pray scriptures. According to Isaiah 55:11, "God's Word will not return empty." When we claim his promises and pray according to his will, he will accomplish his desires. I believe God hears our prayers and then saves them for the right time to answer.

Our descendants do not inherit salvation. Nevertheless, we can pray our descendants will live in a constant awareness of God's presence and be firmly established in His Word, which will prepare their hearts for the time when they are presented and opportunity to step into a personal relationship with Jesus Christ.

We read in Proverbs 14:26, "He who fears the Lord has a secure fortress, and for his children it will be a refuge." Jennifer Kennedy Dean also says, "As we seek the Lord ourselves, we are laying up treasures for future generations by the way God is reflected in our lives. As we invest in our own walk with the Lord and our prayers for our grandchildren and future generations, we are investing in eternity."[4] Now that is a great investment return all of us would enjoy seeing.

"As for me, far be it from me that I should sin against the lord
by failing to pray for you"
(1 Samuel 12:23).

"Do not store up for yourselves treasures on earth, where moth
and rust destroy, and where thieves break in and steal. But store
up for yourselves treasures in heaven, where moth and rust do
not destroy, and where thieves do not break in and steal. For
where your treasure is, there your heart will be also"
(Matthew 6:19–21).

Study Guide
For personal reflection or group discussion

- What responsibility comes with new grandchildren?
- Do you ask your grandchildren about their frustrations, dreams, fears, concerns, and expectations?
- How many generations does it take for a family's faith to be lost?
- Which truths would you like to pass on to your grandchildren?

- How can grandparents threaten the enemy (Satan)?
- Why should you pray for your grandchildren individually?
- Do you have a spiritual trust fund for your grandchildren?

Prayer

Dear Lord, thank you for my family. Give me a greater passion to pray for them. Satan is seeking to destroy our families; however, help me to be intentional in my praying for them. May all those generations who come after us find us faithful. In Jesus' name, amen.

Share Your Ancestral Lineage with Your Grandchildren

Everybody's biological ancestry includes two parents, four grandparents, eight great-grandparents, sixteen great-great-grandparents, and on and on through the generations. What do you know about any of your ancestral lineage? What kind of people were they? Where did they live? What did they believe?

Grandparents' Link to Grandchildren

Families are scattered. They do not all live in the same area as they did years ago. Therefore, it is our responsibility to let our families know about their ancestral lineage. Perhaps, as grandparents, we are the oldest in the family, so we are a vital link between our grandchildren and the preceding generations. The events of our lives, our parents' lives, and of those generations before us make up the blueprints of our lives. If we do not tell our children and grandchildren about their roots, how will they know? How are we affecting the family blueprint for future generations? Do our children and grandchildren know their family stories and history? Have you shared stories and pictures of your family from previous generations? Does your family know your life story? Do they know when you invited Jesus Christ into your heart?

Write a story about what you remember of your parents or grandparents as well as your own story to share with them. Be sure to pass along family pictures when you share it with them. You might also take out a map or show them on a globe where you lived, where your grandparents lived, and where your ancestors came from. I found it interesting to read stories about my ancestors, their struggles in Europe before coming to America, and their challenges of starting new lives as immigrants in a new country in the late 1800s. I soon realized my ancestors were real people, making a life for themselves and future generations like me.

Preserve Your Family Roots

The importance of family is encouraged when we preserve our roots. When we are diligent to preserve our family history, we pass on to future generations an understanding of who they are. Very often younger generations are not interested in listening to stories of family history until they are older. That is why it is important to put these stories in writing so that they will be available when they are interested and those who know are no longer around.

If your family has a Christian heritage, it is important to write about that so succeeding generations can see how powerfully God has worked in your family. If you do not have a Christian heritage, but you are walking with the Lord now, you have changed the blueprint for future generations. Now, that is exciting and worth passing on!

Impress God's Truth and Values

God commanded Moses to tell the Israelites to "Love the Lord your God with all your heart ... Impress them (these commandments) on your children. Talk about them when you sit at home and when you walk along the road, when you lie down and when you get up" (Deuteronomy 6:5, 7). This command is for parents and grandparents. We are both responsible to impress God's truth, values, and purposes upon the hearts and minds of our children and grandchildren by our talk, our actions, and our prayers.

One generation telling its story to another is powerful. Grandparents will contribute much to a grandchild's life by sharing their stories. However, a godly example and prayers make a greater impact. Grandparents living in God's grace and love open the way for the Spirit of God to perform his transforming work in the lives of their grandchildren and keep the legacy alive through their story!

Ask God to show you how you can share your family history with your family. Pray for each member of your family to know and walk in God's grace and truth and for generations yet to be born to continue the legacy of life in Christ.

What Does the Dash Represent?

When I go back to Oklahoma to visit family, I like to go to the cemetery to visit the grave sites of my parents and grandparents. As I was looking at my grandmother's tombstone, I read:

Maria Wiebe
March 7, 1880 – June 14, 1959

Have you ever thought about what the dash between the date of birth and the date of death represents? It represents the lifetime of a person. As I was looking at her tombstone, a memory of my grandmother that quickly came to my mind was that she was a godly woman who loved the Lord and her family. I often found her reading her Bible, serving the Lord by teaching Sunday school, and participating in the women's group at church where they were quilting, sewing for relief organizations, and helping missionaries.

My grandmother followed the commandments Moses gave the Israelites in the desert by teaching me about God and His Word. She lived with my family the last fifteen years of her life. As a small child, one of my favorite times was sitting on the porch swing in rural Oklahoma in the summertime, listening to my grandmother tell me Bible stories and sing Sunday school songs with me in the evenings.

Life was hard for my grandmother as she faced many disappointments and challenging times. Her steadfast faith in Jesus Christ carried her through those difficult years because she loved the Lord with all her heart. When I think of the dash on my grandmother's tombstone, I am reminded of the spiritual impact she had on my life.

Ask yourself:

- When my life has passed what will the dash on my tombstone represent to my grandchildren?
- Will they remember my love for Jesus?
- Will they remember that I was their prayer warrior?
- Will they remember that I walked with God through the valleys and over the mountains on my journey of life?

or

- Will they remember the expensive gifts I gave them or the trips I took them on?
- Will they remember that I did not have time for them?
- Will they say, "I don't remember my grandparents telling me they were praying for me?

Study Guide
For personal reflection or group discussion

- Why is it important for you to share stories of your parents and grandparents?
- If the younger generation isn't interested in hearing about their ancestors, what can you do to preserve your family roots?
- How can you impress God's truth, values, and purposes upon the hearts and minds of your grandchildren?
- What will the dash represent on your tombstone?
- Do you think it can strengthen your grandchildren to hear about the hard life you lived compared to today?

Prayer

Dear Heavenly Father, I thank you for my grandchildren. Help them to remember my love for You and that I have been their faithful prayer warrior. I pray they will recognize that you have walked with me through the valleys and over the mountaintops in my journey of life. Show me how you want me to impress on them your great love for them. In Jesus' name, amen.

"Know therefore that the Lord your God is God; he is the faithful God, keeping his covenant of love to a thousand generations of those who love him and keep his commands" (Deuteronomy 7:9).

"One generation will commend your works to another; They will tell of your mighty acts. They will speak of the glorious splendor of your majesty they will tell of the power of your awesome works, and I will proclaim your great deeds" (Psalm 25:4–6).

Section II

Standing in the Gap with Intercessory Prayer

"I urge, then, that requests, prayers, intercession and thanksgiving be made for everyone … This is good, and pleases God our Savior, who wants all men to be saved and to come to a knowledge of the truth" (1 Timothy 2:1, 3–4).

"But the love of the Lord remains forever with those who fear him. His salvation extends to the children's children of those who are faithful to his covenant, of those who obey his commandments"
(Psalm 103:17, 18, NLT).

Standing in the Gap for Children Other than Your own Grandchildren

Why should the blessing of a praying grandparent be limited to his or her own grandchildren? We have the opportunity to stand in the gap for many children in our churches, as well as children of acquaintances who do not have praying grandparents. I have found that God has placed people in my life because He wants me to pray for them.

Jesus Had a Heart for Children

Jesus had a special place in his heart for children, and if we want to have a heart like Jesus, we will have a heart for children. Jesus tells the disciples, "Let the little children come to me and do not hinder them, for the kingdom of God belongs to such as these" (Mark 10:14).

Children today are growing up in an increasingly hostile world, receiving many conflicting messages through a media-driven culture that is trying to capture their minds. We cannot shelter them from the world, but we can stand in the gap for them and pray a hedge of protection around them.

A Surrogate Grandchild

In 1989, when Patty was fourteen, she and her parents immigrated to the United States from Colombia, South America. Soon after their arrival, my husband and I became friends with her family. Patty asked if we would be her surrogate grandparents. We were delighted to accept the role. We have been praying for Patty as she has gone through high school, college, and medical school. There are many miles between us, but we stay connected with telephone calls, e-mails, and prayer. What a blessing for us to be a part of her life.

Patty wrote us, "You are a gift from God; God has poured His love on me through your support of prayer and love. Your prayers are constant reminders that God knows what we need and meets us where we are. Your prayers have made a difference in my life. I have been blessed in knowing that I have grandparents and they are praying for me."

We have had several opportunities to be involved in the lives of other families. For a number of years, we have been mentoring a young family with three children. Their three children do not have grandparents; however, God has given us the privilege to be their praying grandparents.

God has multiplied our family

Leslie Needham Johnson was two years old when my husband and I befriended her family. She writes the following story. I hope it will encourage you to stand in the gap for some children who are not your grandchildren.

> "I've never felt like a surrogate regarding the way John and Lillian have shown love to me. For as long as I remember, I have had three sets of grandparents. The place in my heart where I hold my deceased grandpar-

ents is the same location I hold my Papa John and Mama Lil. I have so many fond memories with my grandparents, and just the same with my "surrogate grandparents," although it feels funny to call them that.

They say it takes a village to raise a child, and my grandparents took that to heart. They took it so seriously that most of my friends don't even know that there is no blood relation. It is funny because often in the Christian community we hear people say that he or she must have had a praying grandmother when a young man or woman turns out to have a heart for the Lord. I can say that a large part of my heart for God is directly connected to the presence of Papa John and Mama Lil in my life, not only as people who pray for me, but also as grandparents who are consistent. The love God has for us has been demonstrated well through the love these people have shown my family and me.

When I look back over my life, I see my Papa John and Mama Lil never missing the big things and fully enjoying the little things. One of my favorite childhood memories includes them. We would have family dinners where we would go to their house or they would come to ours. These meals consisted of three of my favorite things: Mama Lil's salad (which I now include in my family recipes and make for my husband), yummy cookies, and best of all, Papa John "measuring" how much I learned in school that day. He would tell me to put my arms straight down, and he would pick me up by my fists and see if my brain was heavier than last time. I loved this so much.

This past year on my wedding day I was especially blessed to have surrogate grandparents. My Mama Lil was in the room with my bridal attendants and me as I got ready for my wedding. She was right there with me in the limo ride to the most exciting yet scariest moment of my life, and she was right there in the front row with my Papa John and parents to once again pray for and bless a huge moment in my life.

I am so grateful that today I can write that Papa John and Mama Lil not only saw me as a little girl in their "village," but as a real part of their family."

Children Need Praying Grandparents

Recently I visited with a young mother with four small children, all under six years of age, who attend the church I attend. She is a very busy, stressed mother with no family to help with the children, her husband being in a demanding career. I shared with her about my passion to encourage grandparents to pray for their grandchildren. She shared with me that her children do not have grandparents praying for them. As a result, I asked her to give me the names and ages of her children and said I would pray for them. It challenges me to think there are children in our churches and among our acquaintances who do not have the support of praying grandparents.

We can also pray for the grandchildren or the grandparents of people we read about in the newspaper who have been in accidents or involved in criminal activities. Have you thought about praying for the families of crime victims? Have you thought about praying for the brokenhearted family members whose child or grandchild has died in an auto accident or committed a crime?

My husband and I have been delighted to see God working in the lives of those for whom we have been praying. When we see our prayers answered in the lives of others, we are humbled and encouraged in our own faith. God has blessed us with the privilege to stand in the gap for these dear children, and this has literally expanded our family. It can be a vital ministry.

Study Guide
For personal reflection or group discussion

- Are you standing in the gap for a child who is not your own?
- Are there children in your church who do not have praying grandparents?
- Are you praying for the children in your neighborhood?
- Has God placed some children in your life who need a praying surrogate grandparent?

Is Your Grandparenting a Blessing or Painful?

Grandparenting is a special blessing but can also be painful. Messy family relationships can leave grandparents hurting, depressed, discouraged, and hopeless. Divorce, drugs, alcohol, and adult children who walk away from their faith cause broken hearts for grandparents.

Grandparents are always excited when they learn they are going to be grandparents, especially when they are waiting for their first grandchild to be born. The average age of first-time grandparents is forty-seven.

The babies are so cute and lovable. My friend Susan enjoyed just watching her precious baby granddaughter sleep so peacefully. Her smiles warmed Susan's heart, and later she loved to hear the baby laughing. This grandbaby then became a toddler, running into Susan's arms and bringing so much joy. Susan could hardly wait to teach her granddaughter about Jesus and take her to church. Then she was told by her son, "We do not want you to talk to her about Jesus." Susan and her husband's hearts broke. They had been waiting for the opportunity to teach their granddaughter about their faith. This story is repeated often. Many grandparents have been told they are not to teach their grandchildren about Jesus.

One grandparent told me that her son said to her she could not see her grandchild again because the child told him "Grandma wants to take me to Sunday school." Her son didn't believe in God anymore, so he didn't want his child to learn about Jesus. Closed doors to grandchildren cause broken hearts and relationships.

I have a friend whose son and his girlfriend had a fourteen-month-old boy. They went on a trip for a couple of days and left the baby with the girlfriend's parents. The couple died in a car accident while on their trip. Since the girlfriend's parents were caring for the child, they thought they were in charge of the child and alienated the father's parents' time with the child. The father's parents had to go to court to be able to have time with the child.

The pain is very difficult because it causes a rift between the child's parent and the grandparents. The grandparents lose one of their greatest joys in life. The hurt is compounded when there is a spiritual separation between the child's parent and the grandparent. When an adult child rejects his parents' faith, the parents feel a rejection from the adult child. The pain is suffocating.

Alienation is painful and takes a significant toll on grandparents, especially as their friends are enjoying their grandchildren. A grandparent's pain is often private; they feel they have failed in raising their adult child, which then reflects on themselves. Or your grandchild's parents are going through a divorce and your adult child does not get custody, making it more difficult to have time with the grandchild.

Brokenhearted/estranged grandparents have two choices:

1. They think they can walk away from the pain and fill their lives with other things, but the pain will still be there. 2. They can pray, asking God for direction and peace as they seek his guidance for reconciliation.

I have two suggestions if you are a brokenhearted and/or estranged grandparent: Pray, pray, pray, using Scriptures when praying for your grandchildren, and start or join a Grandparents@Prayer intercessory prayer group.

Grandparents@Prayer is an excellent, safe place for grandparents to share their concerns with other grandparents. My group met this week. Some grandparents shared their broken hearts with us, feeling safe to shed their tears for their grandchildren. We prayed with them and will continue to pray for them in the days ahead, carrying their burden, as Paul tells us in Galatians 6:2. (To learn more about Grandparents@Prayer, see the Appendix.)

We cannot change others or our circumstances, but we have a powerful God. He loves our grandchildren and their parents more than we do.

- Pray that God will be displayed in your circumstances.
- Give God the responsibility to fix the situation. He will do a better job. We often burn the bridge of communication when we try to do the fixing.
- Trust God to fix it in his time, in his way.

Don't let the enemy allow you to become obsessed with your hurting issues. Give them to Jesus. If you are obsessed with your pain, then the enemy has the victory. Trust God to wrap his arms around you and provide you with peace as you wait for him to answer your prayers. While you are waiting, God may be working but you may not be aware of it. Ask God if reconciliation is possible, even though you don't think you have done anything wrong. Asking for forgiveness may be the beginning of healing.

We learn the most from God when life is hard, and

we have to trust him. We often forget that the same God we enjoy in our mountaintop experiences is walking with us through the valleys of our lives.

Many hurting grandparents are raising their grandchildren because the parents are ill, in the military, in prison or various situations, especially today with the opioid epidemic. When parents are absent or unable to raise their children, grandparents are often the ones who step in. Raising a second generation brings many struggles, along with rewards, including the fulfillment of giving your grandkids a sense of security, developing a deeper relationship with them, and keeping the family together.

As grandparents age, raising children can be challenging. Taking care of ourselves mentally, physically, and spiritually is vital to our overall health and our ability to live prosperous lives and raise healthy grandchildren.

Generations United cites a 2013-2015 study by the Casey Foundation, saying around 2.6 million grandchildren are being raised by their grandparents. The 2010 Census showed that about eight percent of all grandchildren under eighteen are living with grandparents. That number grew by about 30 percent from 2009. Now, ten years later, who knows what it is, especially with the opioid issues among millennial parents.

The CDC estimates more than 42,000 people overdosed on opioids in 2016. Fentanyl-related drugs are one of the primary reasons. The opioid epidemic is showing no signs of slowing down in the United States, with deaths from opioid-related overdoses now outpacing car accident fatalities. https://www.healthline.com/health-news/deaths-from-opioid.

If you know grandparents who are raising their grandchildren, pray for them. Many say they feel alienated and lonely because they don't seem to fit in anywhere. Many are retired on a fixed income and find raising the grandchildren very challenging financially, as well as physically and emotionally. Often they are raising their grandchildren because the parents' lifestyle doesn't allow them to raise their own children.

Some hurting grandparents have children and grandchildren in the military. Often grandparents have a big part of raising their grandchildren when either the mother or father or both are deployed. If you know someone who has a loved one in the military, ask them how you can pray for them, especially if their loved one is deployed. It is especially hard for them when their loved one is wounded or will not be coming home.

I am thankful I am not an estranged grandparent, but my heart breaks when I hear the stories of many grandparents who have broken hearts.

If your adult child has walked away from their faith, you are not alone. Many grandparents share your heartache. Try to keep open communication with your child. Let them know you love them and pray for them even though you do not accept their behavior.

Study Guide
For personal refection or group discussion

- What are your options if you are an estranged grandparent?
- What should you do if you don't approve of your grandchildren's behavior?

- What can you do to help your friends who are struggling with their grandchildren's behavior or estranged from their grandchildren?
- How can you encourage grandparents who are raising their grandchildren?
- There are many hurting grandparents. Start a Grandparents@Prayer group, a safe place to share your broken hearts. See Appendix for details.

Prayer

Dear Father, thank you for the grandchildren you have given to us. I pray they will experience your presence with them, even though their home is not a happy, safe place at times. Give the grandparents who are raising their grandchildren physical and emotional strength, wisdom, and provisions to do the best they can under the circumstances. Help me live a godly example before my grandchildren so they will want to walk with you. In Jesus' name, amen.

"He heals the brokenhearted and binds up their wounds"
(Psalms 147:3 NIV).

"The Lord is close to the brokenhearted and saves those who are crushed in spirit" (Psalms 34:18 NIV).

A Look at Our Grandchildren's Culture

Our grandchildren are facing a different culture or environment than many of us did when we were growing up or when we were raising our children. People make culture and are molded by culture. It changes with the generations just as modernization, fashion, and ideas do.

As grandparents, we feel the culture is trying to steal our grandchildren and their parents with its subtle and often dangerous enticements. We read in John 10:10, "The thief comes with the sole intention of stealing and killing and destroying." (PHILLIPS) We are experiencing the thief's subtle intention as we observe the culture/environment our grandchildren are navigating today.

A friend of mine told me about a weekend she spent with her grandchildren. She was appalled to hear the things they were talking about and the amount of time they spent on their cell phones texting their friends. They didn't want to play games with her anymore, only their games on their cell phones. Spending time with our grandkids gives us ideas about how to pray for them.

It is hard for us to accept their behavior, such as body piercings, tattoos, long hair, music, disrespect, dishonesty, and more. However, it is crucial that we let them know we love them even when we do not accept their behavior; they are facing many subtle messages from their friends. It's vital that we model a biblical world view to show them how to live in an immoral world.

I have condensed some
Cultural issues our grandchildren have to navigate from A Practical Guide to Culture
John Stonestreet & Brett Kunkle, *A Practical Guide to Culture*, David C. Cook Publisher, 2017, p 153–155.[1]

The Information Age: The digital revolution has changed our lives. Google has replaced the World Book Encyclopedias. Our grandchildren don't know that we had telephones with cords or televisions with only a few channels, all in black and white, when we were growing up. That was our norm, but it is not their norm. Today's culture makes it difficult for our grandchildren to know which messages to trust in the vast amount of information they receive on their cell phones. Grandparents can create an environment where the grandchildren will feel safe to ask questions about issues they are facing.

Identity: The Bible states we are made in the image of God, and we have to know God to know ourselves. We don't know who we are if we don't know God. Our grandchildren have to deal with transgender bathrooms. My granddaughter's girlfriend suddenly decided she wanted to be a boy, wore boys clothing, and acted like a boy. We are told that even kindergarteners are exposed to gender identity and told they can be either a boy or a girl, whichever they decide.

Pornography: The Covenant Eyes website offers the following statistics: 90 percent of boys and 60 percent of girls said they were exposed to pornography before the age of eighteen. One out of every eight online searches and one out of every five mobile searches is for porn. Pornography takes up one-third of the internet's bandwidth. I know this is heavy, but this is what our grandchildren are facing. Porn produces many consequences. Our grandchildren are told many lies about porn, such as it is harmless and no one else's business. Pray that God will protect the eyes of our dear grandchildren and give them the strength to flee from the temptation of porn when they are enticed.

Addiction: Our grandchildren's minds are filled with lies about legalized marijuana, alcohol, and drugs. It's important they are taught the consequences of using these before they are exposed to them. The use of alcohol and drugs is significant among high school students and higher among college students, and the numbers are rising. Addiction is a result of the emptiness of the soul, and it doesn't take care of the pain. Only their faith in Jesus Christ will give them fulfillment.

Entertainment: Entertainment vies for the souls of our grandchildren in movies, television, music, and video games. Ask your grandchildren about the movies they are watching, and then talk about them. These types of entertainment aren't all bad. However, it is vital that grandchildren are taught how to evaluate them.

Affluence & Commercialism: Our grandchildren are exposed to and influenced by a world of affluence, commercialism, and entitlement by the media today. Our goal should be not to shower them with material wealth but teach them to work for and earn the things they want. Expose them to children living in poverty to familiarize them with how others are surviving. The Samaritan's Purse Christmas Shoebox project is an excellent way for them to participate in helping children less fortunate. Help them to discover that money isn't going to bring them long-term happiness.

Sexual Orientation: The Gay and Lesbian Movement is an issue of our time. Our children are exposed to it at an early age in their families and in school. Homosexuality attempts to exchange their God-identity with self-identify. It's important that we dialogue on this issue with our grandchildren to influence them with the biblical view. We must teach the truth and engage with grace.

Racial Tension: Christians must be cautious not to get absorbed in the racial views of our culture. Our origin as God's image bearers outweighs our ethnic backgrounds. Don't let the world view control your conversations about racial issues. God has created all people in his image; we just have different colors of skin.[1]

Witchcraft: Wicca is among the fast-growing religions. Wicca has effectively repackaged witchcraft for millennial consumption. Wicca's website is one of the most visited religious sites on the internet. All forms of witchcraft are strictly forbidden in the Bible as being tied to the occult and the work and world of the evil one. "Let no one among you who practices sorcery engage in witchcraft or cast spells. Anyone who does these things is detestable to the LORD" (Deut. 18:10–12). Regrettably, culture has made witchcraft mainstream. Talk with your grandchildren and their parents about this subject so they will be able to recognize the witchcraft often placed subtly in some movies and music. (This information was taken from Crosswalk.com, written by Dr. James Emery White, 02-19-2019.)

Daniel's story

Daniel was taken from his home country in Judah to captivity in Babylon, a very ungodly environment. Daniel was to be trained to serve in the king's palace. He resolved not to defile himself with the royal food and wine. King Darius decreed that no one could pray to anyone other than himself for thirty days. Daniel went to his room and prayed three times a day facing Jerusalem, giving thanks and praying as he always did to his God. He did not allow the worldly king to transform him into the pattern of Babylon. As a result, Daniel was thrown into the lion's den. God closed the mouths of the lions, and Daniel was brought out without any wounds because he trusted God. King Darius acknowledged that the God of Daniel was a living God.

Shortly before Jesus was arrested, he prayed for his disciples, asking God to protect them, and I believe it is for us too. "I'm not asking you to take them out of the world, but to keep them safe from the evil one" (John 17:15 NLT).

So, grandparents, there is an urgency to pray intentionally for physical, emotional, and spiritual protection as our grandchildren and their parents navigate the world today. The greatest long-lasting gift we can give our children and our grandchildren is an intentional, praying grandparent.

Study Guide
For personal reflection and group discussion

- Have you listened to your grandchildren visiting with their friends or cousins the same age?
- Have you asked your grandchildren how their friends feel about gender identity, marijuana, pornography, and other cultural issues?
- Ask your grandchildren how they think about cultural issues.
- Have you asked them if they have answers for when they are confronted with culture issues?
- Have you talked with your grandchildren about the racial tensions in school or in their community?
- Have you asked your older grandchildren how you can pray for them or asked the parents of the younger ones how you can pray for them?
- Tell your grandchildren that you are daily praying for their protection physically, emotionally, and spiritually.

Prayer

Dear heavenly Father, protect our grandchildren from:

- Becoming addicted to alcohol, cigarettes, drugs, gambling, pornography, or other forms of addictions.
- Believing the lie that Jesus is nothing more than a good teacher.
- Being lured into "It must be okay if everyone else is doing it."

- Wandering aimlessly, without a purpose in life.
- The enemy's traps, and when necessary, protect them from themselves.
- Being charmed and intertwined in witchcraft, divination, magic, the world of fascinations, and the occult.

In Jesus' name, amen.

"Don't copy the behavior and customs of this world, but let God transform you into a new person by changing the way you think. Then you will learn to know God's will for you, which is good and pleasing and perfect"
(Romans 12:2 NLT).

God's Gift of Intercessory Prayer

"Pray for each other so that you may be healed"
(James 5:15b).

God has given us a gift of intercessory prayer. An intercessor is one who intercedes in prayer on behalf of others. When we love others, we will want to intercede for them. We are responsible before God to pray for those God brings into our lives, which includes our children, grandchildren, and future generations.

Our prayers can prepare their hearts to hear, receive, and understand the truth, God's Word. We open the door for God to work in the lives of our grandchildren when we pray deliberately on their behalf. However, they still must choose to cooperate with God. Be sensitive to the times when you can ask them how you can pray for them.

By the time we get to the autumn season of our lives, we have had experiences in which we have found it hard to pray for ourselves. I have had many difficult times in my life where I found it hard to pray for myself. It felt like Jesus was giving me a hug when my family or friends told me they were praying for me.

Our friend, Donna Lyn writes, "We see the slogan 'Support Our Troops' on bumper stickers and banners across our country, yet what does it really mean? I found out firsthand when my husband, an engineer and Navy Reservist, was deployed to serve in the Middle East for eight months. Our church rallied around our family and bridged the gap while my husband was gone.

"As a wife and mother of four precious children, you would think I would be able to fervently pray for my husband, but I could not. All my life I have had a gift for strong intercessory prayer, but when it came to my husband serving in the war, it was too close to home and too terrifying. Of course, I prayed for him with the children daily; however, the faithful prayer warriors of our church interceded for our family in a personal and practical way to 'Support Our Troops.'

"It was such a comfort for me to know both my husband and our family were covered in prayer by our church. So many times during those challenging eight months of single parenting, I would feel a wave of peace settle over me—as if someone had slipped a warm blanket over my shoulders. I just knew someone was praying for me. The next time you see the bumper sticker 'Support Our Troops' or hear about the war on television, think about the gift of intercessory prayer. Your prayers for the troops and their families will make a big difference for them."

Do you know someone in the military from your church or community you can pray for by name? Ask God how he would have you support those in the military and their families. When we support their spouses and children with our prayers and kindness, we are supporting our troops and honoring God.

Struggling Teenagers of Deployed Parents

Ask your grandchildren if they have friends whose parents are in the military. If they do, encourage them to pray and reach out to their friends and their friends' families with kindness. We are all part of the family of God. We are to share each other's troubles and problems by being intercessors.

Recently, I read an article in *Parade Magazine* about the struggles of our deployed soldiers. I read, "When mothers and fathers are deployed overseas, their children are also in danger. A new report from the Rand Corporation suggests that teenagers in military families suffer much higher rates of emotional distress than other teens. Across all age groups and genders, soldiers' children had significantly greater emotional difficulties."[1] The older children are more aware of the dangers their deployed parents are facing each day.

How to Pray for Military Personnel and their Families

- Pray for grandparents of the children left behind by deployed parents to provide spiritual covering, encouragement, and an intentional ministry of hope in Christ to their grandchildren.
- Pray the grandparents will be able to give the support these children need during this difficult time in their lives, especially the teenagers.
- Pray for the grandparents to be strong as they face the uncertainty and anxiety of their sons, daughters, and possibly grandchildren in potential danger daily.
- Pray the grandparents to have wisdom and direction as they support the spouses and grandchildren left behind.
- Pray for peace for the families as their soldiers face both physical and spiritual warfare in these foreign and hostile environments.
- Pray for comfort and consolation for those who have lost their loved ones or have wounded loved ones coming home.

In addition, I am sure you have family members,

friends, or acquaintances who are going through difficult times with a broken marriage, health issues, family issues, prodigal children, etc. Sometimes, when we are going through these times, the pain is so hurtful that we cannot pray for ourselves. When you pray for others, you open the door for God to work in their lives.

Grieving Grandparents

Many grandparents are grieving for their grandchildren in or out of the military. God has given us the opportunity to carry each other's burdens. Paul tells us, "Share each other's troubles and problems, and in this way we obey the law of Christ. If you think you are too important to help someone in need, you are fooling yourself, you are really a nobody" (Galatians 6:2, 3, TLB). My friend, Peggy Powell, shared these intercessory prayer needs for grieving grandparents with me. "Pray for the heart broken grandparents whose grandchildren are dealing with the following issues:

1. Extremely or terminally ill
2. In drug recovery
3. In rebellion
4. Posted as missing children
5. Flirting with worldly temptations
6. Not in Sunday School
7. Not walking in truth
8. Not in homes that honor Christ as Savior
9. In prison
10. In war zones
11. In a "far country"
12. Hooked on porn

13. Selfish and/or arrogant
14. Not in church
15. Dishonor their parents
16. Neglected or abused in any way[2]

Communicate your prayer support to your grandchildren and others by sending an e-mail or a text message, calling them on the telephone, or sending a written note to let them know you are praying for them. It will bless and encourage them to know you are praying for them. God will bless you for your obedience.

Study Guide
For personal reflection or group discussion

- What is an intercessor?
- Are there people in your church going through difficult times for whom you could pray?
- Are there families in your church who have someone in the military?
- Are there grandparents in your church grieving over the lifestyle of their grandchildren you could pray for?
- When you pray for others, do you communicate your prayer support to them?

Prayer

Almighty and gracious God, hear our prayers for grandparents all over this world who are grieving for their grandchildren. Remind them, O Lord, of Your eagerness to daily bear their burdens. Bring each grandchild " home" to Jesus, as Redeemer, Lord, Provider, and Sustainer. In Christ's great name, amen.

The Gift of Time for Grandparents

Each day God gives us a valuable gift of time. However, we are accountable for how we choose to use this precious commodity. Often, we find ourselves saying, "I can't believe this month is almost over" or "Our grandchildren are growing up so fast." There are situations we will never have the opportunity to relive since our grandchildren grow up so fast. If we do not choose to embrace and enjoy them while they are growing up, we may reach the end of our lives with regret. We are responsible to use our time wisely, since our time is not redeemable.

How do you think God wants us to use our time in relation to our grandchildren? In Psalms 71:18 (NLT) we read, "Now that I am old and gray, do not abandon me, O God. Let me proclaim your power to this new generation, your mighty miracles to all who come after me." As grandparents, we are to use our time wisely proclaiming God's power and miracles to our grandchildren and future descendants. We are to share about the good and difficult lessons God has taught us in our journey of life.

Quality Time for Our Grandchildren

One way to use our time wisely is to pray for our grandchildren specifically every day. Even though we may be retired, it takes an effort to carve out a time each day to pray for them. We need more than a mood; we need to set an appointment, a special time to pray for them intentionally, not just when we feel like it.

Spending quality time with our grandchildren is another way to use our time wisely. Life can get so busy with our own activities and travels that sometimes we have to make a deliberate choice to make the effort to spend time with them.

Busy or Fruitful

Being *busy* is defined as "engaged in action or full of activity." Being *fruitful* is defined as "yielding or producing fruit, bringing results." There is a difference between being busy and being fruitful. Our lives are full of many responsibilities; however, sometimes we must examine our motives and ask ourselves, "Why am I doing this? Am I doing it for selfish motives, or am I doing it out of obedience to God?" God is waiting for us to ask him, "How do You want me to use my time wisely in relation to my grandchildren?"

Satan steals our joy if we choose to be too busy to invest our lives in our grandchildren. Satan's priorities are to distract us with busyness so we will not be effective, godly grandparents. We will be tired, overworked, and stressed. He wants us to be too busy to pray intentionally or take the time for our grandchildren

Recently I read that often our grandchildren will not have time for us when we get older if we do not have time for them when they are young. Time spent attending their little league games, programs, plays, dance or piano recitals, etc. will be well spent. Grandchildren always appreciate their grandparents taking time to be their cheerleaders. Our not carrying through on good intentions to participate in their activities brings only regret later.

Our young granddaughters love to come to our house to visit, especially when Grandpa joins our tea parties or they get to stay overnight. Sometimes it takes a lot of work and energy to make that happen, but it is such a blessing to see their excitement. I often run out of ideas of what to do when they come to visit, but I have found that, whenever I ask, God always gives me ideas.

King Solomon wrote in Ecclesiastes 11:1 (NIV), "Cast your bread upon the waters, for after many days you will find it again." I think that holds true when thinking about our time in praying and spending quality time with our grandchildren. I would encourage you to cast your bread upon your grandchildren. Influence their lives with your prayers and a godly role model. Be a good example and wise in using time, being productive, and not wasteful with the valuable gift God has given you. It will be a wise investment of your time, even if you do not see the fruit in your lifetime.

Study Guide
For personal reflection or group discussion

- How do you think God wants you to use your time in relation to your grandchildren?
- What does Psalm 71:18 tell us about our responsibility as grandparents?
- Is it easy to take time to pray intentionally and specifically for your grandchildren?
- When you are busy, are you always fruitful?
- What are Satan's priorities?
- Is it hard to continue to pray for your grandchildren when you don't see results?

- Do you spend your time in ways that fulfill God's purpose?
- Would God want you to make some adjustments?
- What specific changes would God want you to make to fulfill your responsibility?

Prayer

Lord, show me how to balance my time wisely. Forgive me for the many times I have wasted your precious gift. I choose to invest more time reading and meditating on your Word. Guide and direct me to use my time wisely to fulfill my responsibility as a grandparent. Help me to deliberately pray and spend quality time with my grandchildren. In Jesus' name, Amen.

"My times are in your hands; deliver me from my enemies and from those who pursue me"
(Psalm 31:15 NIV).

Ask God for the Little Things

Today, there is urgency for grandparents to stand in the gap for their grandchildren. I hope this book is challenging you to intentionally intercede for the next generation with your prayers and by the example you are living before them.

Grandparenting is more than giving gifts to your grandchildren. God has given you a responsibility along with the blessings of enjoying these dear ones. There are times we do not know what that responsibility looks like; however, God has given us the avenue of prayer. In addition to praying for your grandchildren, you can ask God to give you wisdom in connecting with your grandchildren. As you pray, do you ask God for little things, or do you just ask Him to do big things for you? Often we think God does not care about the little or insignificant concerns we have; however, He does care about the little things we are concerned about, such as parking places, etc. The little things can weigh heavy on our hearts, so we can get distracted from placing our thoughts on the Lord. He is waiting for us to ask Him for our needs and for the desires of our hearts, little or big, if they are according to His will. When He answers the little things we pray for, our faith grows, and we become more confident to ask Him for the bigger requests we bring to Him.

God Gives Wisdom

For example, I find it rewarding whenever I ask God to give me wisdom regarding a birthday gift for my grandchild. He gives me an idea, and the grandchild is happy about their gift. I have seen God answer my prayer, and my faith grows. We read in James 1:5, "If you need wisdom—if you want to know what God wants you to do—ask him, and he will gladly tell you. He will not resent your asking." He is waiting for us to ask him for the desires of our heart. Otherwise, we can waste our precious time trying to come up with our own answers.

God wants us to develop an intimate relationship with him so we can feel comfortable asking him specifically for our concerns for our children, grandchildren, and ourselves. He desires for us to bring our most intimate desires to him. We need to be honest with Him about our feelings, our longings, our needs, and our wants. If we have resentment, forgiveness, or other sins in our lives, it puts up a wall between God and us. However, if we confess our sins, God is faithful to forgive our sins and cleanse our hearts.

Ask for the Right Motives

As we grow into a more intimate relationship with the Lord, we will bring our concerns for our children and grandchildren with a right motive. We read in James 4:3, "When you ask, you don't get it because your whole motive is wrong — you want only what will bring you pleasure." Our motives may be for our own benefit, not how God would want to answer our prayers. We must have an open mind and ask God how He wants to answer our prayers. Sometimes we do not recognize the answer to our prayers because God has answered them differently than we thought He would or should.

Do not underestimate the power of prayer for your

children, grandchildren, or yourself. When we realize the power of prayer, our faith will increase, and it will give us more confidence and boldness in our praying.

Study Guide
For personal reflection or group discussion

- How do you think God wants you to use your time in relation to your grandchildren?
- What does Psalm 71:18 tell us about our responsibility as a grandparent?
- Is it easy to take time to pray intentionally and specifically for your grandchildren?
- When you are busy, are you always fruitful?
- What are Satan's priorities?
- Is it hard to continue to pray for your grandchildren when you don't see results?

Prayer

Dear Father, help me to grow into an intimate relationship with you so I will feel comfortable asking You for the little things that concern me for my children and grandchildren. Show me if I have any sin in my life that might hinder my prayer life. In Jesus' name, amen.

A Grandmother's Prayer

Dear God, I am grateful for the grandchildren you have given me. I pray you will give me the grace to be a "Grammy" who loves, accepts, leads, and guides them with your love. I want to model my faith in Jesus so they will be encouraged to put their faith in you early in their lives. I pray they will develop a compassionate heart with a desire to serve others.

When discouraged, may they trust you for their hope for a future and develop perseverance during hard times. May they enjoy hard work and find joy and contentment in each day, despite difficult circumstances. Help them to enjoy the small things in their lives, taking time to smell the roses and notice the beautiful clouds in the sky. I trust they will seek new experiences in your creation around them in place of material possessions. I pray they will hold their possessions loosely and give cheerfully to your work. My desire is for them to develop a strong prayer life as they grow in their faith. Above all, may they seek your guidance in everything they do and may Jesus' love shine through them to everyone. In Jesus' name, amen.

Written by Joy Boschman, California, 2009

God's Timetable vs. My Timetable

Does your timetable match God's timetable? In John chapter 11, we read about the death of Lazarus where Mary and Martha sent word to their dear beloved friend Jesus to let him know their brother Lazarus had become very ill. They expected Jesus to come heal their brother, but he did not come. Disappointed, they wondered why.

However, Jesus had a different plan. He told the disciples, "This sickness will not end in death. No, it is for God's glory so that God's Son may be glorified through it." He loved Mary, Martha, and Lazarus very much, but stayed in Galilee teaching and healing the sick on His timetable.

Two days later, Jesus told his disciples it was time to go to Judea to see Mary, Martha, and Lazarus. On his arrival, Jesus found that Lazarus had already been in the tomb for four days. Martha said to Jesus, "If you had been here, my brother would not have died."

Mary's Response to Jesus

Nevertheless, Jesus went to the grave deeply moved, asking to have the stone removed from the tomb. Martha said, "But Lord, by this time there is a bad odor, for he has been there four days." Jesus told her, "Did I not tell you that if you believed, you would see the glory of God." Then Jesus prayed to the Father and called out in a loud voice, "Lazarus, come out," and Lazarus came out of the tomb. After Lazarus rose from the dead, many who had come to be with Mary and Martha placed their faith in him.

Mary and Martha were disappointed because God did not answer immediately. However, think of all the people Jesus had the opportunity to heal and teach during those two days, with many believing in him. Jesus, God's Son, knew the Father's plan and His timetable. It was not God's plan to heal Lazarus when he was sick. He wanted to glorify his Son by raising Lazarus from the dead.

He is Still on Time, Even When We Think He is Late

Our finite minds simply cannot grasp God's infinite ways of answering our prayers. We have no idea how many times He is waiting on us for the proper time to answer. Sometimes God needs to work in our hearts, our character, or another person before He can answer our prayers. When we get discouraged and impatient, we have to remind ourselves that God's timing is always perfect, since He knows what is best for us.

I just talked with a friend on the telephone who has been praying for a prodigal grandchild to come back to the Lord. It is hard to wait for the prodigal's return, but we have to continue in prayer, waiting for God's timing.

God Glorified

Another lesson we can learn from John 11 is that God allows bad circumstances in our lives, which we do not understand, so that He will be glorified. I had an issue in my life that upset me and caused resentment in my heart, and I did not understand why God allowed it to happen to me. After struggling with the issue for several months, God directed me to John 11. He showed me that He could use bad events in my life to reveal his power and purpose so He would be glorified.

Study Guide
Personal reflection or group discussion

- Does your timetable match God's timetable?
- Was Jesus on time for Mary and Martha when Lazarus became ill?
- Can our finite minds grasp God's infinite ways of answering our prayers?
- What lesson can we learn from the story in John 11?
- Is God's timetable too slow for me sometimes?
- Am I getting tired of waiting on God to answer my prayers for my grandchildren?
- Am I disappointed and frustrated because God is not answering in my time?
- Does God want to develop character in my life or in the lives of my grandchildren before he is ready to answer?
- How do I respond when God does not answer my prayers according to my plan?

Prayer

Dear Heavenly Father, help me to trust You and develop patience as I wait for you to answer my prayers. Help me to remember that you are working, even though it does not appear so to me. Help me to remember that you see the overall picture and know what is best for me. In the name of Jesus' amen.

A Grandfather's Prayer

Dear Heavenly Father, Your Word proclaims that children are a gift from God. My children have blessed me with many grandchildren, and I thank you for each one. I pray that I will carry on your hope to our future generations. My prayer for each grandchild is that they will experience your fullness in their daily walk with You. May they desire to live for You, guard their steps, and draw near to You, experiencing your love for them. In times of testing may their hearts and minds be drawn to you, causing them to remember your Word, and give them a way to escape as you promise. In addition, help them to honor you through the life you've given to them. Help me, as their grandfather to reflect a clear image of You through the life you have given to me. I trust You to give me patience and love to influence, and encourage them into your grace. I commit each one of my grandchildren into your care and blessing. In Your precious name, I pray, Amen.

Written by John Penner, Oregon, 2009

"Children are a gift from the Lord; they are a reward from him" (Psalm 127:3 NLT).

"Children's children are the crowning glory of the aged" (Proverbs 17:6 NLT).

Lillian Ann Penner

Seedtime and Harvest for Grandparents

During springtime when we see the daffodils and tulips blooming, we often think of preparing our gardens. I grew up on a farm in the Midwest, and we always had a garden to grow our own potatoes and vegetables. As I was thinking about sowing seeds in the garden, I was reminded of the fruit of the Spirit in Galatians 5:22, 23 (TLB), "But when the Holy Spirit controls our lives, he will produce this kind of fruit in us: love, joy, peace, patience, kindness, goodness, faithfulness, gentleness, and self-control."

When we invite Christ into our lives, the seed for the fruit of the Spirit is sown into our hearts. A life controlled by the Holy Spirit will exhibit the character traits of the fruits of the Spirit.

To produce a good crop, the seeds need watering, sunshine, weeding, and pruning. When our grandchildren enter into a personal relationship with Jesus Christ, the Holy Spirit comes into their hearts, preparing the soil for the seed to be sown in their hearts. Along with the sun, the soil needs watering with God's Word for the seed to sprout and grow. Jesus the Son of God must shine on their hearts for the plants to grow. After the weeding and pruning have taken place, the seeds will produce a good crop.

We can aggressively pray, knowing it is God's will for godly seed to be sown in the lives of our children, grandchildren, and future generations. The seeds of prayer we plant today will yield a harvest of blessing in the future. God has given us a powerful resource in the avenue of prayer to bring power and blessing to their lives as well as ours. Just as God told the Israelites, "I will pour out my Spirit on your offspring and my blessing on your descendants," (Isaiah 44:3) God will pour out his blessings on our lives when we sow seeds of prayer.

Pray:

- Your grandchildren will allow God to prepare the soil of their hearts.
- Your grandchildren will invite Jesus Christ into their hearts.
- Their hearts will be watered with God's Word for the seed to grow.
- They will allow the Holy Spirit to control their hearts.
- They will experience God's presence and love in their hearts when being weeded and pruned with disappointments in the challenges of life.

Study Guide
Personal reflection or group discussion

- What needs to happen before a life will exhibit the character traits of the fruit of the Spirit?
- What results will the seeds of prayer bring to us?
- Use God's Word when praying for your grandchildren.
- Pray through the suggestions on the following pages for the fruit of the Spirit.

The seeds of prayer you plant today will yield a harvest of blessing in the future.

Fruit of the Spirit

As our grandchildren, grow in their relationships with Jesus Christ; allowing the Holy Spirit to control their lives, they will produce a harvest of the fruit of the Spirit manifested in their lives.

Suggestions to Pray for the Fruit of the Spirit

Love

Love is an intense feeling of tender affection and compassion. It is unselfish, loyal, and benevolent concern for the good of another.

- Ask God to plant His love in the hearts of your grandchildren so they will be aware of His presence at all times.
- Pray they will invite him into their hearts and be rooted and established in His love and His Word.
- Pray they will allow God's love to flow through them to their families, friends, and others.

Joy

Joy is a feeling of great pleasure. It is to delight in something. It is also evoked by well-being and success.

- Ask God to plant a joyful heart in your grandchildren.
- Pray they will find joy in being successful in school and their other activities.
- Ask God to enable them to experience the joy of the Lord as their strength, especially when going through difficult circumstances.

Peace

Peace is a state of calmness and quiet. It is freedom from disturbing thoughts of emotion. When one experiences peace, he or she feels secure and in harmony with their personal relationships.

- Ask God to plant His presence in the lives of your grandchildren so they will grow strong and have quiet, calm spirits in their hearts.
- Pray they will experience God's peace, even when going through difficult situations.
- Pray that God's peace will overflow from their hearts to others.
- Pray they will feel secure in their family and school situations.

Patience

Patience is the capacity to be patient, showing self-control, or bearing pain or trials without complaining. It is being calm, steadfast, and persevering, even while waiting.

- Ask God to plant patience in the hearts of your grandchildren, as He refines them to become all He wants them to be.
- Pray for them to have patience when waiting for God to answer their prayers because very often their timing is not God's timing.
- Pray they will learn to be patient and tolerant with their family members and friends.

Kindness

Kindness is having compassion and sympathy, being gentle, thoughtful, considerate, and helpful.

- Pray for your grandchildren to choose to sow seeds of kindness, since kindness is a deliberate action.
- Pray they will look for places to plant seeds in random acts of kindness.
- Pray they will be kind, thoughtful, considerate and helpful with family members and with their friends and classmates.

Goodness

Goodness is being kind, friendly, well behaved, admirable, honest, sincere, and of reliable character.

- Pray your grandchildren will choose to have goodness in their hearts.
- Pray your grandchildren will sow seeds of goodness to others.
- Pray your grandchildren will be well behaved and of reliable character.

Faithfulness

Faithfulness is being true, real, loyal, trustworthy, reliable, and committed.

- Pray your grandchildren will see God's faithfulness to them and grow strong in their spiritual lives.
- Pray they will be able to place their complete trust in God.
- Pray they will be dependable, reliable, loyal, and trustworthy and do what is right.

Gentleness

To be gentle one is tenderhearted, calm, kind, quiet, peaceful, and well mannered.

- Pray your grandchildren will have a tender heart with a gentle spirit.
- Pray your grandchildren will have a calm, peaceful spirit and be well mannered.
- Pray they will be considerate of the feelings and needs of others.

Self-Control

To have self-control one needs to have self-discipline, willpower, restraint, and the ability to control one's own behavior, especially in reactions and impulses.

- Pray our grandchildren will desire a heart of self-control.
- Pray they will learn to control their behavior and their tongues.
- Pray they will recognize when Satan is tempting them and wants to steal their hearts.
- Pray they will use self-discipline to stand firm in the Lord.

Pray for Your Grandchildren's Parents

Our children have a great responsibility parenting our grandchildren in these insecure, unstable times we live in today. Young families are busy with their jobs, church activities, children's activities, etc. There are many distractions for them in their marriage, employment, and parenting.

In today's broken world, Satan's purpose is to destroy the family. It is important that we pray God will give our children wisdom and time management in their monumental task of guiding our grandchildren in the ways of the Lord.

Study Guide
For personal reflection and group discussion

- Who has the primary responsibility of parenting your grandchildren?
- Where do grandparents fit in the parenting of the grandchildren?
- Why is it a difficult job for the parents?
- Who is trying to destroy the family unit today?
- Discuss the issues parents have with their children at different age levels.
- Pray the prayer on the following page for your grandchildren's parents.

Prayer

Dear Lord, first, I want to thank you for the parents of my grandchildren. Help my children to value their children in the same way You value them. I pray they will commit to the responsibility You have given them to teach their children to love You and train them according to your parenting manual, God's Word. Give our children wisdom to manage their time so they will be able to take the time to teach our grandchildren the ways of the Lord. Give them wisdom in how to nurture and care for the children. I pray they will be loving and caring parents. May the children see their home and family as a "safe place." Help them to rule their home well, not provoking the children to anger. Help them to be fair and understand the children as You understand us. Pour out your Spirit upon my children as they parent my dear grandchildren. Bless their homes. In Jesus' name, Amen.

A Prayer for a Granddaughter

Adapted from I Peter 3:3, 4 and Colossians 3:12–17
(Insert child's name.)

Dear heavenly Father, I pray _____ will not be concerned about the outward beauty that depends on fancy hairstyles, expensive jewelry, or beautiful clothes, but that she will clothe herself with the beauty of a teachable, gentle spirit, displaying pure and godly behavior, for this is precious in Your sight. I pray _____ will have a balanced view of beauty and charm, clothing herself with attractive and modest apparel, radiating the countenance of a godly young woman, choosing to dress in a way that pleases You. I pray _____ will clothe herself with tenderhearted mercy, kindness, humility, gentleness, and patience, making allowances for the faults of others and forgiving those who offend her. But the most important virtue is love. Let the peace that comes from Christ rule in _____'s heart. I pray the words of Christ will live in _____'s heart and make her wise, so whatever she says or does will be pleasing to God. Moreover, I pray _____ will grow up to be a godly woman, loving You and serving You all the days of her life. In Jesus' name, amen.

A Prayer for a Grandson

Adapted from Proverbs 6:20–23 and I Peter 5:6–9
(Insert child's name.)

Dear Lord, I pray my dear grandson,_____
will obey your commands, and not neglect the
teachings of his mother and father. Keep your words
always in his heart and tie them around his neck.
Wherever he walks, your counsel will lead him.
When he sleeps, you will protect him. When he
wakes up in the morning, you will advise him.
Your Word is a beam of light directed into the dark
corners of his mind to warn him of danger and to
give him a good life. I pray _____ will cast
all his anxieties on You because You want what is
best for him. I pray _____will recognize the
temptations and deceitfulness of the enemy, Satan.
Be self- controlled and alert, resist the enemy,
standing firm in his faith. Keep him from the
immoral behavior of the world he sees in person,
in print, in the media or on the computer. Lord, I
pray _____ will grow up to be a godly man
who loves you and serves You as long as he lives. In
Jesus' name, Amen

Praying God's Word for Your Grandchildren

We become very aware of the spring season if we live in the areas where we experience the four seasons. Spring reminds us of new life when we see new buds on the dormant winter trees and see the bulbs pop out of the ground almost over night.

During the winter, many areas experience very cold, harsh weather. However, as spring approaches, it gives us the hope of warmth and beautiful gardens and landscapes. As it warms our spirits, we become alive and more energetic.

We often go through seasons in our prayer lives where we do not take the time to read and meditate on God's Word or to pray intentionally for our grandchildren or ourselves as we should. We pray, but our prayers may become humdrum, repetitive, or pointless.

That was my experience a number of years ago when I felt the prayers for my grandchildren were very general and superficial. Being a long-distance grandmother, I prayed they would be safe and have a good day, and I would be on my way. I felt my prayers became rote, empty, and powerless.

God Gave Wisdom

However, that all changed after I asked God to give me wisdom and insight on how I could pray for them intentionally. Praying intentionally means a determination to pray in a certain way, done by intention or design. However, after I asked God for direction and read several books about prayer, I was encouraged, and I gained some tools to help me to pray intentionally and regularly for my grandchildren and their parents.

I discovered God's Word was a great resource to help me with my praying, not only for my family, but also for myself. In Hebrews 4:12 we read, "The Word of God is alive, and powerful it exposes our innermost thoughts and desires." In her book, Jennifer Kennedy Dean writes, "Prayer is simply opening our lives to God, acknowledging our total dependence on Him, living in the presence of God, always in the process of being reshaped and recreated by Him."[1]

When I pray according to God's Word, I am in line with His will. This enables me to pray with direction, power, and wisdom. As I claim God's promises and personalize the scriptures, I experience more confidence and boldness in my praying.

Many scriptures in Psalms, Proverbs, the gospels, and Paul's writings can be used in our prayers. I believe God *loves* to hear us verbalize His Word back to Him when we pray. Here is an example: "I have hidden your word in my heart that I might not sin against you" (Psalm 119:11). "Dear Lord, I pray Sam will remember the Scriptures he memorized in his Awana Club and that they will come to his mind when he is tempted."

Praying: An Intimate Relationship with God

In praying scripture, I not only find myself in intimate communication with God, but my mind is being renewed to think His thoughts about the situation for which I am praying, instead of my own thoughts. Ultimately, God shrinks the situation that I thought was overwhelming and impossible to a viable possibility. He gives me peace as I wait for His answer.

As we start claiming God's promises and personalizing the Scriptures, we experience more boldness and confidence in our praying. Nothing threatens the enemy (Satan) more than when we are intentionally praying God's Word for our children, grandchildren, and ourselves.

If you are in a "winter" season in your prayer life and you have not been spending time with the Lord regularly in prayer, allow the spring season to bring new life to your prayers.

Prayer

Dear Father, as I am reading your Word, show me the Scriptures I can pray for my family and myself. Help me to set an appointment with you each day and show me how you would like me to be an intentional prayer warrior for my family. In Jesus' name, amen.

In the Appendix in the back of this book, you will find "Scriptures to Pray for Your Grandchildren" for each day of the month, along with "Prayers from God's Word," to help you to pray intentionally for your grandchildren.

Prayer from Romans 12 for Your Grandchildren
(Insert your grandchild's name.)

Father in heaven, I pray _____ will:
- Love sincerely and not fake it.
- Run for dear life from evil.
- Stand on the side of the good.
- Be a good friend.

- Take delight in honoring others.
- Never be lazy in his/her work, but serve the Lord enthusiastically.
- Be glad for all God is planning for him/her.
- Be patient in trouble.
- Always be prayerful.
- Help needy Christians.
- Be hospitable.
- Bless his/her enemies.
- Be happy with others when they are happy.
- Share their sorrow, if they are sad.
- Get along with others.
- Not be stuck up or arrogant. Never think he/she knows it all.
- Not pay back evil for evil or hit back.
- Discover beauty in everyone.

In Jesus' name, amen.

Prayer Adapted from Ephesians 1:17–23

(Insert grandchild's name)

Dear Father, I ask you, the God of our Lord Jesus Christ, to give_____ spiritual wisdom and understanding to grow in his/her love for you. I pray that the eyes of _____'s heart will be flooded with light so that he/she can know the hope and glorious future you want to share with him/ her. I pray _____ will begin to understand how incredibly great your power is to help those who believe in you. I pray _____ will realize that the same mighty power that raised Jesus from the dead and seated him at your right hand is available to him/her today. In Jesus' name, amen.

Prayer Adapted from Psalm 119:33–38
(Insert your grandchild's name.)

Dear Lord, I pray you will give _____ a soft, teachable heart for your Word. Give _____ understanding of your Word and a desire to obey your instructions for living. Direct to walk along your path, for that is where he/she will find happiness. Give _____ an eagerness for your principles, rather than a love for money! Turn _____'s eyes from worthless things, and help him/her live in Your ways. Fulfill your promises to _____ because he/she loves You. In Jesus' name, amen.

Prayer Adapted from Colossians 1
(Insert your grandchild's name.)

- *Lord,* help _____ to always remember to give thanks to you.
- Build in_____ a strong faith in you.
- Fill _____ with knowledge of Your will in all wisdom and understanding.
- Teach_____ to walk in a manner which pleases You.
- Help _____ to be strengthened with Your power for attaining steadfastness and patience.

- O God, may_____ honor You as the One who created all things for yourself.
- I pray that You will have first place in _____'s life.
- May You, Father, make_____'s faith strong, stable, and fixed on the truth of the gospel.
- Proclaim in _____'s heart the glorious truth, "Christ in you, the hope of glory." In Jesus' name, amen.

Strolling Through Ephesians Praying for Your Grandchildren

Strolling through Ephesians, we bump into a bunch of "bees."

Be holy and blameless. (Eph. 5:27)
Be completely humble and gentle. (Eph. 4:2)
Be patient. (Eph. 4:2)
Be made new in the attitude of your mind. (Eph. 4:23)
Be kind and compassionate to one another. (Eph. 4:32)
Be imitators of God. (Eph. 5:1)
Be strong in the Lord. (Eph. 6:10)
Be very careful, live as a wise person. (Eph. 5:15)
Be alert and always keep on praying. (6:18)

Prayer

(Insert your grandchild's name.)

Loving Lord, I pray You will create in _____ a thirst to please You. May _____ choose to imitate you—walking in harmony with your will in personal integrity and in relationships with people. I ask, Father, that You continue to build into _____ holiness, humbleness, gentleness, and patience. Keep_____ developing and growing in kindness, compassion, wisdom, and strength. I pray, O God, that You would help_____ be alert and aware of danger and develop a habit of prayer. In Jesus' name, amen.[2]

Section III

Standing in the Gap for the Grandchildren

"The child grew and became strong; He was filled with wisdom, and the grace of God was upon him. Jesus grew in wisdom and stature and in favor with God and men" (Luke 2:40, 52).

Grandchildren Going Back To School

The school bells ring every fall for many of our grandchildren. The beginning of the school year can be a stressful experience for grandchildren with new teachers and new classmates, especially if they are going to a new school setting. They may also have to adjust to new coaches, bus drivers, car pools, and other situations. Our grandchildren are growing up and being educated in a time of uncertainty. They are subject to pressures and temptations many of us did not experience in our youth; however, we can pray for their protection from the deception the world offers and that their eyes will be blinded to the temptations they face in school.

Pray for Protection

Satan is trying to steal our children away from walking with God. Jesus says, "The thief's purpose is to steal, kill, and destroy. My purpose is to give life in all its fullness" (John 10:10 NLT). However, we have the opportunity to pray for their protection from Satan and his demons and for them to experience the fullness of the Lord in their lives. When we long for those hugs and kisses and think of how much we miss our grandchildren, it is a good time to say a prayer for them.

Prayer

Dear Lord, I pray my grandchildren will:
Desire to do their very best.
Respect their teachers.
Choose friends who will have a positive influence.
Recognize the deception of worldly thinking.

Have eyes blinded to the temptations they face.
Have a balanced view of their beauty, charm, and strength.
Learn to be responsible for their actions and behavior.
In Jesus' name, amen.

Send a Back-to-School Note

For the last few of years, I have sent my grandchildren *back to school notes,* telling them that we will be praying for them as they start a new school year. They may be facing frightening or uncomfortable situations as they attend new schools, have new teachers, and make new friends. A note of encouragement from their grandparents may give them the confidence they need as they go back to school.

Grandma Sets her Alarm

I heard of a grandmother in Texas who sets the alarm on her cell phone each day at the time each of her grandchildren are going to school to remind her to pray for them.

Pray for the Adult Influences on Your Grandchildren

Have you thought about praying for the many adults who influence your grandchildren? Are the adults involved in your grandchildren's lives good role models?

Adults who have influence on your grandchildren may be their other grandparents, teachers, principal, coaches, carpool or bus drivers, Sunday school teachers, children's directors, pastors, youth leaders, neighbors, scout leaders, extra-curricular activity teachers, doctors, etc. Many other adult influences indirectly affect our grandchildren, including elected and appointed officials, (local, state, and federal), TV producers, developers of electronic games, musicians, textbook authors, members of the media, fashion designers, etc.

Ask your grandchildren for their teachers' names, and, if possible, meet their teachers and others involved in their lives so you know for whom you are praying. It makes praying more personal if you have an opportunity to tell them you are praying for them.

Prayer

Dear Father, I pray the adult influences of my grandchild will always speak the truth, model lives of integrity to the children, and transport the children safely, looking out for the children's best interest. I pray they will make the children feel safe, protecting them from verbal, emotional, and physical abuse. I pray they will be encouragers to the children, live blameless lives, do what is right, and speak the truth with a sincere heart. In Jesus' name, amen.

Pray for Grandchildren to be Known by their Actions in School

"Even a child is known by his actions, by whether his conduct is pure and right" (Proverbs 20:11).

- Pray your grandchildren will learn to follow instructions and conduct themselves with right behavior.

- Encourage your grandchildren to be obedient to their parents.
- Help them to understand that being well behaved is pleasing to God, their parents, teachers, and others. Appropriate behavior will be beneficial to them.
- Help them to understand that sometimes it is hard to be good, but God will help them to make right choices for appropriate behavior, if they ask Him.
- Pray they will have gentle, kind, and honest words.
- Pray that your grandchildren will recognize when they are tempted to sin, think about it, and choose to resist the enemy.
- Pray that if they do sin, they will admit it, confess the sin to God, and ask forgiveness, if they have hurt another person.
- Pray also they will learn to think before they speak and choose their words wisely.

Pray for Your Grandchildren to Have Success

"People who despise advice are asking for trouble; those who respect a command will succeed. If you ignore criticism, you will end in poverty and disgrace; if you accept criticism, you will be honored"
(Proverbs 13:13, 18 NLT).

"If you listen to constructive criticism, you will be at home among the wise. If you reject discipline, you only harm yourself; but if you listen to correction, you grow in understanding"
(Proverbs 15:31, 32 NLT).

Grandchildren need to learn to accept advice and constructive criticism. Those who accept guidance and correction will be successful in life. They only hurt themselves when they do not accept correction.

Pray your grandchildren will accept and respect advice from their parents, teachers, and those in authority over them, so they will be prepared for life's experiences.

Pray for Your Grandchildren to Control their Tongues

The way our grandchildren respond to others is important. Getting along with others is a big part of having success in school, relationships, and in their work experience. Learning to get along with one's siblings is a good place to learn to get along with others. Learning to control anger will keep your grandchildren from making some big mistakes. Pray your grandchildren will:

- Learn to control their tongue at an early age for success in their relationships with their families, in school, and in their places of employment (Proverbs 13:3, NLT).
- Learn to speak gently with understanding and not stir up anger with harsh words, which they will regret, especially in confrontations (Proverbs 15:1).
- Learn to control their tongues when angry. Anger can cause mistakes (Proverbs 14:29).
- Learn that "the tongue of the wise brings healing" (Proverbs 12:18).

Pray for God's Armor of Protection in School

"Finally, be strong in the Lord and in his mighty power. Put on the whole armor of God so that you may take your stand against the devil's schemes" (Ephesians 6:10, 11).

As grandparents, we need to pray our grandchildren will grow strong in their walk with the Lord and learn to put on the armor of God because our culture is challenging their faith. Our younger grandchildren have challenges with lying, cheating, disobedience to parents, etc. Our older teenage grandchildren and our young adult grandchildren need protection, as they tend to push the boundaries of godly lifestyles. The devil is deceptive and he tries to distract them from walking with the Lord.

Study Guide
Personal reflection or group discussion

- Do you think your grandchildren need an extra amount of prayer as they go back to school?
- How can you communicate to them you are praying for them as they go back to school?
- Discuss all the adult influences your grandchildren have as they go back to school.
- Pray they will be known by their positive behavior.
- Discuss why it is important that they are successful in school.
- Discuss the importance for them to learn to control their tongues.

Pray your grandchildren will:

- Recognize the deception of the world.
- Put on the whole armor of God so they are ready to fight their daily temptations.
- Arm themselves with Christ's righteousness by repenting of their sins.
- Stand firm with the belt of truth (God's Word).
- Hold the shield of faith to recognize and extinguish all the flaming arrows of the evil one.
- Memorize the Word of God so the Holy Spirit can use it when needed to withstand the enemy.
- Be alert, self-controlled, and stand firm in their faith.

Pray for Grandchildren to Make Wise Choices

"And this is my prayer: that your love may abound more and more in knowledge and depth of insight, so that you may be able to discern what is best"
(Philippians 1:9, 10).

The lives of our grandchildren are full of decisions. Peer pressure can make it hard for our grandchildren to make the right choices, even though they know what is right and best. Our grandchildren need to learn at an early age that Jesus is waiting for them to ask him to help them make the right choices. Encouraging the children to learn and memorize God's Word will help them to stand firm, to know what is right, and to refuse the wrong.

It is never too early for us to pray for our grandchildren regarding crucial choices and turning points in their lives, especially as they become teenagers. From our experience, we know how early decisions shape a person's life in important ways—choice of friends, educational choices, career moves, marriage partners, and which church to attend.

Make Good, Deliberate Choices

Our grandchildren must make deliberate choices to avoid the ungodly attitudes and influences of this world. A discerning heart is one that is perceptive to godly choices. Most of us, in either our immediate or extended families, have dealt with painful situations caused by wrong choices: an out-of-wedlock pregnancy, a drug charge, a car accident caused by drunken driving, intimidation by gang members, failing grades due to negative influence of peers, and/or school discipline problems due to rebellious behavior.

"Sometimes grandparents tend to think they know how things should turn out for their children or grandchildren. Only God knows what truly is best for those we love. Let's ask the Holy Spirit to guide our prayers according to his plan for them as they make important choices."[1] However, our grandchildren will have to choose to cooperate with God.

Encourage your grandchildren to make wise choices by reflecting godly qualities in their life that differentiate them from the world in today's godless society.

His divine power has given us everything we need for life and godliness through our knowledge of him who called us by his own glory and goodness. Through these, he has given us his very great and precious promises, so that through them you can participate in the divine nature and escape the corruption in the world caused by evil desires
(2 Peter 1:3–4).

Study Guide
Personal reflection or group discussion

- Who are the biggest influences on our grandchildren other than their families?
- What are some of the choices they have to make?
- What kind of heart is perceptive to godly choices?
- How can grandparents influence their grandchildren to make wise choices?

- How do wrong decisions influence a person's future?
- How can you encourage your grandchildren to hide God's Word in their hearts so it will be there when needed in the future?

Pray your grandchildren will choose:

- To have a personal relationship with God.
- To live in such a way as to find favor with God and man.
- To be careful how they live and make godly choices.
- To accept what is right and reject what is wrong.

"Be very careful, then, how you live—not as unwise, but as wise, making the most of every opportunity"
(Ephesians 5:15)

Pray for Grandchildren to Choose Friends Wisely

"The righteous man is cautious in friendship, for the way of the wicked leads them astray"
(Proverbs 12:26).

The friends of our grandchildren can have a great impact on their lives especially when they get to school and in their teenage years. Their peers and education influence their lives more than anything else, except for their home and family.

Who is My Friend?

As I was reflecting on my friends, I asked myself, "What makes someone my friend?" I determined that a friend is someone who accepts me just the way I am, believes in me, and encourages me; someone who is trustworthy and loyal, who forgives my mistakes, enjoys being with me, and makes me laugh.

Friends are important to a child's healthy development. It is not emotionally or spiritually healthy for a child to be isolated. If your grandchild does not have close friends, pray that God will bring him or her good, close friends. We all have a natural desire to be a part of something that gives us a sense of acceptance and affirmation.

The quality of friends is more important than the quantity. As grandparents, we can pray they will develop godly, courteous, trustworthy, honest, and helpful friends, not based on how attractive, smart, clever, or popular they are. Encourage your grandkids to guard their hearts and recognize the characteristics of good friendships. Ask God to place an umbrella of protection (emotionally, academically, physically, sexually, and spiritually) over them in choosing their friends.

It is important that our grandchildren be acquainted with children who have different personalities, abilities, and interests. It is equally important that we encourage them to be friendly and sensitive to the differences of other children.

If we look closely at our grandchildren, I think we will find they are not much different than we are in that they are sometimes attracted to children who have character flaws that do not make them good friend material.

Discernment for a Good Friend

It is vital that your grandchildren recognize that they do not have to be close friends with everyone when they feel uncomfortable in a relationship. However, they should be kind to everyone and not be rude. Grandparents can pray for them in this area and teach them how to recognize when a relationship may have a poor influence on them. Pray for them to have discernment and strength to separate themselves from anyone who is not a good influence. Many times when they make wrong choices, it is because they are seeking someone's approval or acceptance, wanting to fit in, especially at school where their peers can greatly influence their lives.

When they get to know a person who is godly and trustworthy, they can begin to share more in depth. It is through these interactions that they can learn to get along with other people and develop meaningful relationships.

Be a Friend Observer

When you are with your grandchildren and their friends, be a good listener and observe them, then compliment your grandchildren on their friend's good qualities when you see them. If your grandchildren live near you, ask them to bring a friend when they come to visit. Last year I invited a couple of my granddaughter's friends for an Easter Tea. The girls dressed up, and we decorated spring hats with flowers, baked and served resurrection rolls, and shared the meaning of Easter. It was a good opportunity to become acquainted with her friends.

If your grandchild has a godly friend who is a good influence and enriches your grandchild, ask God to protect that relationship. However, it is also important that our grandchild be a positive influence on their friends to encourage character development in each other's lives.

Pray for discerning minds and hearts and for God's protection as your grandkids develop their friendships.

Pray your grandkids will see others through the eyes of Jesus.

Expanding the Prayer Circle for Our Grandchildren

My friend, Peggy Powell in Dallas, Texas, sent me this inspiring story from her "Praying Grandmothers" newsletter:

"Some years ago my friend Sandy shared a prayer story that greatly encouraged me. Sandy prayed diligently for her son, Jim, all of his life, but as his teen years began to bud, she found herself travailing, even *begging* the Lord for Jim's protection—especially since Sandy didn't know his new circle of junior high friends, nor their parents. Fears crept in. Doubts about their good influence, much less their godly influence, on Jim appeared in Sandy's mind. One day on her knees, Sandy was imploring the Lord to protect her son from any bad influences of his friends. Suddenly she stopped. She asked herself, "Why don't I pray for Jim's five new friends?" So one by one, she regularly called their names before the Father, praying that they come to know Christ personally and grow in their faith, living lives that honored the Lord.

Within a few months, one of the five became a Christian. In the next year, two more received Christ, and by the time Jim finished high school, four of the five were walking with the Lord.

Sandy continued to pray for each of the boys. Years went by. One day in a grocery store, Sandy was chatting with a young woman who went to high school with her son, Jim, and grew up across the street from Sandy. She asked Sandy, "Have you heard the good news about Bud? He recently became a Christian and is enthusiastically participating in a men's Bible study!" Happy tears flooded Sandy's eyes as she heard the joyful news and prayed right there in the grocery store, "Thank You, Lord, that's all of my boys!"

Where are they now? Every one of Jim's friends is

walking with the Lord. One is a pastor. When Sandy recently visited his church, she had a big surprise. Knowing she would be there, all of "her other boys" came, too. The sweet reunion was truly a celebration of God's faithfulness of her prayers over the many years."[1]

Our grandchildren have many influences in their lives, especially as they enter the preteen, teen, and young adult years. These influences often have a greater influence than their parents or their grandparents. Pray specifically and by name for their peers during this school year.

Like Sandy, we can pray the names of our grandchildren's friends before our Father, praying that each one will come to know Christ personally and grow into spiritual maturity, becoming people who will make a difference for Christ in their generation. Ask your grandchildren for the names of their friends and pray for them.

Study Guide
Personal refection or group discussion

- What makes someone a friend?
- Why are friends important in a child's healthy development?
- What kind of friends do we want for our grandchildren?
- Is it preferable for them to have only a close friend or a group of friends?
- Is it important for them to be acquainted with children with different personalities, abilities, interests, and races?
- Do you know the names of their closest friends?

Prayer

Dear Heavenly Father, You know how easily my grandchildren can be influenced by their friends—the fashions, music, their passions and problems. I ask You to protect_____ and draw each of his/her friends unto Yourself. May Your Presence in the lives of my grandchildren be a clear and consistent witness of your redeeming power to their friends. In Jesus' name, amen.

Challenges Produce Growth in Grandchildren

What a joy it is to have that precious little grandchild come running into your arms with hugs and kisses—the six-year-old calling to tell you she lost her first tooth, your teenage grandson calling to ask if he can come over to visit, or your seven-year-old grandchild, excited about making three goals in his soccer game.

Unconditional Love Wants to Protect

Grandparents love their grandchildren unconditionally. We want to protect them from pain, disappointment, or discouragement. They face many trials and challenges: a friend hurting their feelings, not making the soccer team, a big test in school, or the loss of a job. It does not matter if they are preschoolers, teenagers, or adults; they all face challenges.

Humanly, we want to rescue them by praying, "Don't let anything bad happen to them." However, the Lord may say, "I need to allow disappointment, pain, and failure because I want them to learn to trust me when they are afraid, troubled, or discouraged so I can pour my blessings on them." The Lord has given us a promise to remember when we go through difficult times that we can share with our grandchildren. "Don't be afraid, for I am with you. Do not be dismayed for I am your God. I will strengthen you. I will help you. I will uphold you with my victorious right hand" (Isaiah 41:10 NLT).

Challenges Promote Character

God may allow challenging situations in the lives of our grandchildren for a purpose. Trials and challenges are inevitable; they may be God's invitation to develop character and grow in their spiritual lives. Our grandchildren must learn to expect them, submit to them, and learn from them.

The challenges they face each day are not meant to destroy them. They are designed to make them stronger spiritually, develop character, and make them capable of fulfilling their God-given assignments. Suffering creates an environment where they can see the true nature of their dependency on God. Pain brings us all to the place where we must acknowledge something greater than ourselves. It comes down to whether we believe God and are willing to trust Him in the midst of our challenges and pain. As grandparents, let us not hinder their growth by not allowing them to go through their challenging situations.

David writes, "The Lord will fulfill his purpose for my life" (Psalm 138:8). He had confidence in the Lord's perfect plan, even though there were many difficult and challenging times in his journey. God has created each of our grandchildren for a unique purpose and given us the awesome opportunity to be their grandparents, partnering with Him on their behalf with our prayers.

Study Guide
Personal reflection or group discussion

- What do you enjoy most about your grandchildren?
- Do your grandchildren know if you love them conditionally or unconditionally?
- What does our love for our grandchildren want to do?
- How are character and spiritual growth developed?
- When our grandchildren go through difficult times, is it good to rescue them?
- Do you share with your older grandchildren how God has walked with you through difficult times?

Ask God to help your grandchildren:

- Learn to expect, submit, and learn from their trials and challenges.
- Learn to trust the Lord when they are afraid or troubled.
- Learn to cast all their anxieties on the Lord because He cares for them.
- Understand and accept their God-given assignments.
- Be motivated to pursue those assignments.
- Trust Him to provide the resources to fulfill the assignments

Pray to Guard Their Hearts— God's Treasure

Do you believe God treasures your heart? In John 3:16, NLT, we read, "God loved the world so much that he gave his one and only Son, so that everyone who believes in him will not perish but have eternal life." A treasure is something of great value. God thought our hearts were of such great value that He sent his Son to die on the cross for our sins so we could have a personal relationship with him and spend eternity with him. Since He treasures our hearts enough to die for us, He wants to dwell in our hearts.

Guard Relationship with God

If we really believe God values our hearts enough to give His son to die for us, we must guard our hearts. By guarding our hearts, we protect our relationship with Him. We must choose to abide in Him on a consistent daily basis; it does not happen automatically. He desires us to handle our hearts as His treasure, hold them tightly, and not be careless. We can encourage our grandchildren to allow their hearts to be tender and teachable to God's Word and not to be careless with His treasure.

Our grandchildren are living in the midst of a battle, a brutal and vicious war against a subtle and friendly enemy (Satan) who knows his time is short. We have a responsibility to pray for them and encourage them to guard their hearts. Proverbs 4:23 NLT, says, "Guard your heart above all else, for it determines the course of your life." If we as grandparents guard our own hearts, we will have a part in nourishing the hearts of our dear grandchildren so they will recognize the deception of the world and guard their hearts.

How Do We Guard Our Hearts?

We can protect, defend, and shield our hearts from Satan by developing an intimate relationship with God. Paul tells us, "Set your hearts on things above … not on earthly things" (Colossians 3:1, 2). The enemy wants to rob our hearts; he tries to get us overwhelmed, defeated, tired, and so busy that when God wants to get our attention to communicate with us, His call goes to "voice mail." As grandparents, we can set an example by demonstrating that our relationship with God is a high priority for us.

Vulnerable to temptation

A weak or empty heart is vulnerable to temptations by the devil. Jesus told his disciples, "Watch and pray so you will not fall into temptation. The spirit is willing but the flesh is weak" (Matthew 26:41). When we are tired, discouraged or our hearts are cluttered or divided, we become weak and vulnerable to temptations. If we yield to temptation, God has made a way for us to receive forgiveness. We just need to confess our sin, and then He will forgive our sin, and cleanse our hearts because we are His treasure.

By choosing to spend time in God's Word, and to communicate with Him in prayer, we can strengthen our hearts to live victoriously. Encourage your grandchildren to grow strong in their faith so they will be able to guard their hearts—Gods treasure. Pray your grandchildren will:

- Invite Jesus into their hearts
- Guard their hearts by reading God's Word and learning about Him
- Grow strong in their faith so they will recognize the temptations they face each day

Study Guide
Personal reflection or group discussion

- What is a treasure?
- How does God treasure our hearts and the hearts of our grandchildren?
- How do we guard our hearts?
- Why is it important to guard our hearts?
- What happens to an unguarded heart?
- How can we encourage our grandchildren to guard their hearts?

Prayer for a Clean Heart from Psalm 51:10

Dear Lord, create a clean, pure heart in _____, a heart that desires to trust and obey the Lord. When _____ sins help him/her to acknowledge and confess the sin. Then he/she will experience peace in his/her heart with a clean, renewed spirit. In Jesus' name, amen.

God Provides Protection for Our Grandchildren

"Don't copy the behavior and customs of this world, but let God transform you into a new person by changing the way you think. Then you will know what God wants you to do and you will know how good and pleasing and perfect his will really is" (Romans 12:2 NLT).

Our grandchildren are living in conflict with two worlds, the godly and the worldly. The world is giving them loud and glaring messages to copy its behavior and lifestyle. It is urging them to establish their identity in the things of the world.

However, God has given our grandchildren a way to transform their lives, giving them a godly identity. When they invite Jesus Christ into their lives, they are transformed into new people. Their ways of thinking change as they grow in their relationships with the Lord.

Our grandchildren often feel the principles and boundaries God has given us are hemming them in or holding them back. Even our young grandchildren struggle with the behaviors and customs of the world exhibited through the media, as well as by their friends and peers, especially as they enter school. However, God's principles protect them from a potentiality dangerous lifestyle and give them freedom within the boundaries of the principles God has set up for us in his Word. As they spend time in the Word of God and grow in their relationship with Him, they will know how good and pleasing and perfect His will really is for them.

As grandparents, we can pray they will be protected

from the deception of the world with its customs and behaviors and enjoy freedom within the boundaries God gives in the Bible.

Study Guide
Personal reflection or group discussion

- In which two worlds do our grandchildren live?
- Describe the behavior of each.
- Discuss Romans 12:2, telling us how to live.
- How can grandparents help their grandchildren see that God's principles will save them from a potentially dangerous lifestyle and give them freedom within boundaries God has set up for them?

Pray your grandchildren will:

- Have a personal relationship with Jesus Christ
- Not let the world tell them who they are
- Not copy the behavior and customs of the world
- Not let the world squeeze them into its mold
- Find their identity as a child of God
- Let God transform and shape their inner life, changing from the inside out

Suggestions to Pray for Different Stages of Life

It is important for us to pray specifically and individually for our grandchildren. I often ask God to bless them in one lump sum; however, I think it is good to pray for them individually by name every day. You may want to go to a library and check out a book on the different stages of child development. Following are a few suggestions of how to pray for them in the various stages of life—infants, toddlers, elementary-age, teenagers, young adults, and married grandchildren.

For infants, pray they will:

- Develop a strong sense of security as they bond with their family
- Feel safe and secure in their surroundings
- Grow physically strong and mentally alert
- Begin to lay a healthy foundation for good communication
- Begin to develop a healthy attachment to their family members

For toddlers, pray they will:

- Develop a healthy self-image
- Develop a sense of independence
- Develop a sense of obedience to their parents
- Be willing to try new, unfamiliar experiences
- Feel secure apart from parents (i.e., with caregivers)
- Learn to play independently

For preschool-age grandchildren, pray they will:

- Develop a well-balanced personality
- Learn problem resolution skills
- Play well with others
- Learn to obey quickly, and to respect authority
- Explore and create without fear of failure
- Develop a soft heart towards Jesus
- Develop confidence and independence
- Learn to control their emotions and anger
- Develop an awareness of God's love for them
- Build positive friendships

For elementary-age grandchildren, pray they will:

- Discover their God-given gifts and talents
- Develop a sense of satisfaction and enjoyment using their skills
- Be motivated, disciplined, and challenged in their learning experiences
- Treat others with respect
- Stand firm for what is right and refuse the wrong with a positive attitude
- Choose friendships wisely
- Obey their parents
- Develop a strong and healthy self-esteem and self-confidence
- Have a safe, healthy classroom environment
- Be protected from the deception of the enemy
- Develop a hunger for God's Word

For teenagers, pray they will:

- Be motivated, disciplined, and challenged to apply themselves and excel in their academic studies
- Experience the reality of Jesus Christ in their lives, as they grow strong in their faith
- Recognize the deception of the world
- Be covered with God's safe keeping physically, spiritually, and emotionally
- Date wisely
- Be sexually pure
- Have open communication and a good relationship with parents
- Choose friends who will have a positive influence
- Grow spiritually with a hunger for God's Word
- Have a balanced view of their beauty, charm, and strength

For young adults, pray they will:

- Be motivated, disciplined, and challenged to apply themselves in their studies to excel academically, if they are in college
- Seek God's wisdom and direction in their management of time, money, and talents
- Think creatively and live with integrity
- Recognize their gifts so they can find their God-given assignment
- Provide the resources to fulfill their God-given assignment
- Find a spouse who has a growing relationship with Jesus Christ
- Be sexually pure

- Be willing to accept responsibility and make wise financial decisions
- Have open communication and a good relationship with parents

For married grandchildren, pray they will:

- Understand how incredibly great God's power is to help, if they ask Him
- Establish spiritual disciplines as part of their lives
- Read God's Word and pray together regularly as a couple
- Seek God's guidance in the management of their time, money, and careers
- Develop open and honest communication with their spouse
- Grasp the importance of saying, "I'm sorry" and "I forgive you"
- Understand there is no such thing as too many hugs
- Honor their parents
- Be united in spirit and intent on one purpose
- Be able to stand firm against anything that might threaten their marriage
- Be able to establish a stable, loving, Christian home for their family
- Recognize the deception and peer pressure of the world

Study Guide
Personal reflection or group discussion

1. Discuss the various stages that your grandchildren are going through at this time, and then pray for them.

Connect with Your Grandchildren

Staying in touch with our grandchildren helps us to know how to pray for them. Helen Kooiman Hosier writes in her book, *Living the Lois Legacy,* "Praying about the details keeps us on our toes so that we will know what to pray about, what their needs, hopes, dreams, frustrations, anxieties, fears, concerns, joys, and expectations actually are. Their knowing that we do this kind of praying is a reminder to them to keep in touch."[1]

Sending telegram prayers for our grandchildren when we think of them is a good thing to do, but praying for them deliberately and specifically takes daily discipline. Never underestimate the power of prayer.

Keep in Touch

Letting your grandchildren know you are praying for them is a reminder to them that you love them, want to connect with them, and desire to have a part in their lives. There may be times when our prayers can be more powerful than our presence, especially when they are teenagers and do not have much time for us. God may even say to us, "Do not bug them. Keep your mouth shut about the issues, the music, long hair, and body piercing. Just pray for them and love them." It is important for us to communicate to our grandchildren that we love them and accept them, even though we may not accept their behavior.

Maintain Connection

As our grandchildren enter their teenage years, they may only tolerate us instead of adoring us as they did when they were young. Nevertheless, it is important that we maintain a connection with them during this fragile and exciting time in their lives. Tell your grandchildren how important they are to you and what a privilege it is for you to have them in your life. This is a time when we should focus on their hearts, not on their clothing or hair or tattoos. Ask their parents what would be a meaningful connection with them.

Scriptures with the Alphabet Letters

Another unique way to let your grandchild know how you are praying for them is using the scriptures for the letters of their name, as in the following example. If you need duplicate letters in a name, search the scriptures for another one. You may also want to do this for a child's birthday, Valentine's Day, a new baby card or a friend's birthday.

Sample: Haley

H Humble yourself before the Lord. Philippians 2:3
A Acknowledge God to direct your path. Proverbs 3:6
L Live in harmony with others. Romans 12:16
E Encourage others. Hebrews 3:13
Y Yield yourself to God. Romans 6:13

A List of Verses You Can Use for Each Letter of the Alphabet

A-Acknowledging God who will direct your path.
   Proverbs 3:6

B-Be strong in the Lord. Ephesians 6:10

C-Cast all your anxiety on God. 1 Peter 5:7

D-Do not conform to the pattern of the world.
   Romans 12:2

E-Encourage others daily. Hebrews 3:13

F-Filled with the Spirit. Ephesians 5:18

G-Guard your lips. 1 Peter 3:10

H-Humble yourself before the Lord. Philippians 2:3

I-Invite Christ into your life. John 1:12

J-Joyful-Always be joyful. 1 Thessalonians 5:16

K-Keep your tongue from evil and your lips from
   speaking lies. Psalms 34:13

L-Live in harmony with one another. Romans 12:16

M-Meditate on God's Word. Psalms 145:5

N-Not grow weary in well doing.
   2 Thessalonians 3:13

O-Obey your parents. Ephesians 6:1

P-Practice hospitality. Romans 12:13

Q-Quench not the Spirit. 1 Thessalonians 5:19

R-Renew your minds with God's Word.
   Romans 12:2

S-Seek God first in all things. Matthew 6:33

T-Trust in the Lord with all your heart.
   Proverbs 3:5, 6

U-Understand the Lord's will. Ephesians 5:17

V-Value your personal time alone with God.
   Mark 1:35

W-Work for the Lord. Colossians 3:23
X-Examine your priorities regularly.
   1 Thessalonians 5:21
Y-Yield yourself to God. Romans 6:13
Z-Zealously guard your hearts, for it affects every-
   thing you do. Proverbs 4:23

Have fun!

Electronic Age

Living in this electronic age, enhances our ability to stay in touch with our grandchildren. Today, we can send them a text message, call on the phone, send an e-mail, send cards or an e-card, or visit with them on Skype or other visual media on the computer to keep in touch. Some grandparents get on Facebook primarily to communicate with their grandchildren.

A Texas Grandma Shares an Idea

"I have a holder by my kitchen sink with a page containing names and photos for each of my seven grandchildren. Each grandchild has his or her special day of the week and knows their *day* when I especially pray fervently for them. When Cooper was four years old, I asked him one day, 'Hey, Coop! Do you know what day it is today?' He eagerly answered, 'Yes, this is Tuesday. It is *my* day!' What a blessing it was for me to hear him say he knew it was his day."

Favorite Things

Another way to get to know your grandchildren better is by asking them about their favorite things. Your interest in them will let them know that you are interested in them. You will find a list of "Favorites" to ask them about in the Appendix.

Photo Prayer Journal

A photo prayer journal is a working document to help you pray effectively for your grandchildren, whether you are a long-distance grandparent or live near your grandchildren. You can write what you are praying for them and see how God is answering your prayers. The photo prayer journal will make your praying more meaningful when you see their pictures as you are praying for them.

An example and sample is located in the Appendix.

Mary Shares about Her Photo Prayer Journal

My friend, Mary shared with me that several years ago she read in our churchwomen's newsletter an article where I had shared about my photo prayer journal. The photo prayer journal had a section with a profile sheet and picture for each of her grandchildren, and a page to write her requests. Mary said, "I became very interested in it because I have eighteen grandchildren to pray for and keep track of. Since then I have made my own photo prayer journal. I use it every day, and it has been such a blessing to me."

Communication between grandparents and

grandchildren is unique and powerful. When we take the time to connect with our grandchildren with our love, our prayers, our time, and our example of living for the Lord, our lives will be enriched and full of blessings. As I indicated in an earlier chapter, I found the photo prayer journal very meaningful.

Study Guide
For personal reflection and group discussion

- How do you keep in touch with your grandchildren?
- Do you ask your older grandchildren "How can we pray for you?"
- Do you ask the parents of the younger ones "How can we pray for the children?"
- How do you communicate to them that you are praying for them?
- Do you tell your grandchildren how important they are to you and what a privilege it is to have them in your life?
- Do you use electronics to communicate with your grandchildren, and why is that important?

Suggestions to Pray:

- Ask God to give you opportunities and creative ideas to connect with them.
- Ask God to give you unconditional love for them.
- Ask God to protect your grandchildren from the deception of the evil one (enemy) who is trying to steal them from the Lord.

Seasonal Suggestions for Connecting with your Grandchildren

Valentine's Day

A Valentine's Prayer for Your Grandchild

Dear God, give_____ a good heart:

- a heart that is gentle, tender, and teachable
- a heart that loves You
- a heart that wants to obey You
- a heart You can use for Your glory

In Jesus' name, amen.

A Valentine's Prayer for the Hearts of Your Grandchildren from Proverbs

Dear Heavenly Father, I pray _____ will:

- trust you with all his/her heart
- not depend on his/her own insight
- keep your words in his/her heart
- always have a cheerful happy heart
- listen to the words of the wise
- keep on the right course for life
- reflect your love to the hearts of others
- have a soft, teachable heart
- above all else, guard his/her heart, for it affects everything he/she does

In Jesus' name, amen.

Easter

Easter Ideas

When was the last time you told your grandchildren you are praying for them? Easter is a great time to connect with your grandchildren, whether they live down the street, across town, or far away. As grandparents, God has given us an awesome responsibility and privilege to have a part in the lives of those dear grandchildren. Our prayers and encouragement can make a significant impact on their lives. Let us make Easter a special celebration of the death and resurrection of our Lord Jesus Christ.

Here are a few suggestions you can use during this Easter season:

- Send your grandchildren an Easter card with a Bible verse and/or a note that you are praying for them. Grandchildren enjoy getting mail from their grandparents.
- Send a CARE package: Easter egg coloring kit, Easter craft, Easter paper plates, napkins, and cups for a family dinner, or a storybook with the true meaning of Easter. Of course, Easter would not be complete without some traditional candy.
- E-mail an electronic Easter card.
- Send them "Resurrection eggs." You can purchase them at your local Christian bookstore or online at http://www.christianbook.com.

Memorial Day

In the United States, Memorial Day commemorates the men and women who died while in military service to their country. As we celebrate Memorial Day, let us pray for the families they have left behind. Since the Iraq & Afghanistan wars have begun, there have been over five thousand American deaths. Many families are mourning their loved ones.

In some cemeteries, they place a flag at the grave of all the soldiers who have died in the war. Take the grandchildren on a drive through the cemetery to see all the flags. Pray for:

- Grandparents who have lost their grandchildren in the military service
- Grandparents who are reaching out to their grandchildren, who have lost their parents in the military service
- The loved ones of those who made the ultimate sacrifice for our freedom
- Those loved ones to have the courage to face each day
- Our armed service men and women to be covered with God's sheltering grace and presence as they stand in the gap for our protection

July 4

On July 4, we celebrate Independence Day, the birthday of our nation. Many men and women have fought for the freedoms we enjoy. We often get discouraged with what is going on in our country, but we still have the freedom to pray and worship God. Thank God for the freedom we have in this country to worship God. Take the time to share with our grandchildren how blessed we are to live in America. Have a birthday celebration for our country with your family.

Pray for Truth to prevail and lies to be exposed in our media and our government at the local, state, and national level.

Veteran's Day

When Veteran's Day is approaching, share with your grandchildren about the many people who have sacrificed for the freedoms our country enjoys. Talk about the members of your family that have served in the military. If your grandchildren know someone who is deployed in the military now, encourage them to pray and reach out to that person and his or her family.

Thanksgiving

Thanksgiving is a good time to encourage our grandchildren to be thankful for the many things they experience. Help them make a list of things for which they can be thankful—their home, food, clothing, school, friends, church, toys, and the opportunities they enjoy. Gratitude always improves one's attitude. Send them a Thanksgiving card or call them to let them know you thank God for them, you are thankful they are your grandchildren, and you are praying for them.

My Thanksgiving Tradition

At our family Thanksgiving dinner, when we have our dessert, we place a candle on everyone's dessert plate. Then we light the candle and we go around the table sharing, from the youngest to the oldest, what we are thankful for. We blow out our candle after we share. It has become a tradition and a meaningful family experience.

Christmas

Christmas Gifts Ideas to Enhance Your Relationship with Your Grandkids

A friend of mine gave her granddaughter sewing lessons for her Christmas gift. It did not cost her very much, and they were able to spend quality time together several times. A grandfather might take his grandson fishing or go to a sporting event with him for a gift. Ask God to give you ideas of how you can give them memories that can enhance the relationship.

Family Tradition

Give your family the gift of a tradition of the true meaning of Christmas, which can be passed on to future generations. A tradition in my family was that my parents always read the Christmas story from the second chapter of Luke before opening gifts. My husband and I still do this. I have noticed that my sons are following the same tradition. What a blessing it would be for my parents if they could see that this tradition has been passed on to their future generations.

- What do you want your grandchildren to remember about celebrating Christmas with you?
- Do you want them to remember something about celebrating the true meaning of Christmas, such as

blowing out the candles on Jesus' birthday cake or reading the story of the birth of Jesus from the Bible before opening the gifts?

- Ask God for creative ideas of how you can share the true meaning of Christmas with your grandchildren.
- Have you prayed about the gifts that you are going to give your grandchildren for Christmas?
- Ask God to give you ideas of what you might do to encourage your grandchildren to think of others and their needs, not only their own.

"Commit to the Lord whatever you do, and your plans will succeed"
(Proverbs 16:3).

Christmas Prayer

As grandparents, we have no greater joy than to know our children and grandchildren are walking with the Lord. Pray deliberately for them to walk in the truth, using the following suggestions from the word "Christmas." I pray my grandchildren will:

C - Cast all their anxiety on God because He cares for them. (1 Peter 5:7)

H - Humble themselves before the Lord; he will lift them up. (James 4:10)

R - Renew their minds. (Romans 12:2)

I - Imitate God. (Ephesians 5:1)

S - Seek first God's kingdom and his righteousness. (Matthew 6:33)

T - Trust in the Lord with all their hearts. (Proverbs 3:5, 6)

M - Meditate on God's Word. (Psalms 1:2)

A - Abound in their love for God and His Word. (Philippians 1:9)

S - Stand firm in their faith. (1 Peter 5:9)

Operation Christmas Child

Our grandchildren are growing up in a self-absorbed, "ME" generation, thinking mostly of themselves and what they want or what benefits them.

One way we can teach them to do good deeds is to participate with them in Operation Christmas Child, a project of Samaritan's Purse. Millions of boys and girls around the globe live in difficult circumstances and are in desperate need of hope. It is an excellent way to expose our grandchildren to helping children who are less fortunate and making a difference in another child's life.

My husband and I recently visited our granddaughters, who live in another state, and took them to the store to shop for items to fill a shoebox. They each filled a shoebox with items for a girl their own age. The girls had fun shopping. Their enthusiasm blessed us and gave us an opportunity to talk with them about those who are less fortunate. Since then, every time we go visit them, even out of the Christmas season, they ask if we can go shopping for the shoeboxes. You can get the needed information on this shoebox ministry at www.samaritanpuurse.org

Study Guide
For personal reflection and group discussion

1. Discuss ideas to share God's love with your grandchildren during the different seasons.

Lillian Ann Penner

Christmas Reflections

Reflecting on My Childhood Christmas Tree

Lillian with her Christmas tree, 1943

As I was looking at the forlorn, misshaped tree standing in the snow on the cover of *Grandma's Christmas Legacy,* by Casey Schutrop, I was reminded of the Christmas tree we had at my house when I was a child.

When I was six years old, my parents had very little money to spend at Christmas time. In order for my parents to have enough money to buy me a present, they decided to cut a branch from our juniper tree in the yard for our Christmas tree. I remember at the time I was very disappointed because I thought it was ugly, straggly, and misshapen. I wanted my parents to buy a beautifully shaped tree from a Christmas tree lot in town. However, I recently found a picture taken that year with me standing by the branch tree. After we had decorated it with a garland made of popcorn and cranberries, hung a few ornaments, and silver tinsel, the tree did not look too bad.

Now, when I remember what the straggly juniper branch looked like when my father cut it from the tree and compare it to the beautiful, decorated, well-shaped tree in my home, I see it differently. I see the straggly, forlorn branch as a person's life without God or one depleted from nourishment. I see the beautifully shaped tree in my home as a person's life, filled with God's love and purpose and decorated with ornaments representing the fruits of the Spirit.

God can take a straggly, forlorn life and transform it into a beautifully shaped, fulfilled life. Jesus told Nicodemus, "For God so loved the world that He gave his only Son, so that everyone who believes in him will not perish but have eternal life" (John 3:16). He can change a straggly life into a beautiful new life, a flourishing life, filled with love, peace, and joy, if we believe in him.

Often, our lives become damaged and appear like a straggly, forlorn tree, misshapen by the trials, challenges, and disappointments of life. However, our lives can be transformed into flourishing lives by the renewing of our minds with His Word.

God promises that when we have a personal relationship with Jesus Christ, giving Him every area of our lives, we will take on a true and proper shape. We will become a flourishing tree, pointing others to God.

When you see a Christmas tree this year, I hope it will remind you of the new, everlasting life we have in Christ Jesus, when we invite Him into our lives and trust Him with the challenges and disappointments of life.

Do you feel like a tree that has been twisted, damaged, or made crooked by fears, circumstances, difficulties, or sin? God is waiting to give you new life and fulfillment with nourishment from His Word.

- Ask God to show you, your children, and grandchildren areas you need to humbly submit to the Lord, laying your concerns before Him as the wise men did when they brought their gifts to baby Jesus.
- Ask God to help you, your children and grandchildren turn the damaged, flawed, and misshapen areas of life over to Him.

Reflecting on the Lights of Christmas

As I was reading *Grandma's Christmas Legacy: The Testimony of the Tree,* I was reminded of the twinkling lights we see at Christmas and how God wants us, as His children, to light the world with His love.

It is always a fun family activity to go out in the country to a tree farm or Christmas tree lot to purchase the Christmas tree. Most of our families get into a lively discussion to agree on the perfectly shaped tree. Once we get the tree home, secure it in the stand, and get the tree lights untangled, we are ready to hang the lights on the tree.

We love the Christmas lights, illuminating our homes, and candles lit on the mantle or the dining room table, providing a beautiful, festive atmosphere.

Many of us hang outdoor lights on our houses. We enjoy driving around our neighborhoods to see the beautiful twinkling outdoor lights decorating the houses, trees, and displays.

As you place the strings of lights on the tree this year and enjoy the beauty of the lights in your home and your neighborhood, think about what Jesus commanded in Matthew 5:16. We are to let our lights shine before men, that they may see our good deeds and glorify our Father in heaven.

- How will you illuminate God's love to your family, friends, and your neighborhood?
- What good deeds are you going to do this Christmas to glorify God?
- Pray for your children and grandchildren to stand strong as a symbol of hope in the world today.
- Pray they will radiate God's love and greatness to others.

Reflecting on the Fragrance of Christmas

During the Christmas season, we not only enjoy the beautiful lights of Christmas, we also enjoy the aromas of Christmas. If we have a fresh-cut Christmas tree, we can smell the fragrance of the tree when we walk into the house.

There is also the smell of the holiday-scented candles or spicy fragrances of potpourri when we come into a room, or the smell of wood burning in the fireplace. We love the smells of the delicious cookies, candy, and foods prepared in the kitchen, especially during the Christmas season.

If Christ lives within you, you have the sweet, wholesome fragrance of Christ. Does the fragrance of Christ come from your life?

After several weeks, when the tree dries and does not have enough nourishment, the strong pine tree fragrance diminishes. Very often, we get busy with life and its challenges, and our spiritual nourishment diminishes. Has the fragrance of Christ diminished in your life?

Give God a gift of renewing your heart with His Word so you will leave a life-giving fragrance to your friends and family at Christmas.

Reflect on the fragrance you are releasing to others when you smell the difference fragrances of Christmas. Are you giving forth the fragrance of Christ living within you?

Share with your grandchildren how the fragrances of Christmas remind us of God's life-giving fragrance within us when we have a relationship with Him. Pray for your grandchildren to have the fragrance of Christ within them to release to their family and friends.

I have enjoyed reading Casey Schutrop's book, *Grandma's Christmas Legacy: The Testimony of the Tree.* I think you would, too. This book provides excellent Christmas reading and a memory-maker for families to share and pass on for generations to come.

What Is Your Response to the Birth of Jesus?

After the angels announced the birth of Jesus to the shepherds, the shepherds hurried to Bethlehem and found Mary and Joseph, and the baby lying in a manger. The shepherds were so excited about the angels' announcement they told everyone what they had seen and heard, and all the people who heard the shepherd's story were astonished. Then the shepherds went back to the fields, watching their flocks, glorifying, and praising God for what they had seen and heard. However, Mary quietly treasured all these things in her heart and thought about them often. When the wise men finally found Jesus, they brought expensive gifts and worshipped Him.

When the Christmas celebrations are over, the tree has come down, the decorations put away for another year, what is your response to the birth of Jesus Christ?

Are you glorifying and praising God for sending his Son into the world to save us from our sins?

Are you worshipping the Lord and quietly meditating on His Word?

Study Guide
Personal reflections or group discussion

- What are your Christmas reflections from childhood?
- What Christian traditions are you passing on to your children and grandchildren?
- How do you reflect on the lights and fragrances of Christmas?
- When the Christmas celebrations are over, what is your response to the birth of Jesus?

Don't pack Jesus away with the Christmas ornaments until next Christmas.

Prayer

Pray that your children's and grandchildren's response to the birth of Christ will be one of glorifying and praising God for the new life he has provided. Pray they will stand as a symbol of hope in a dark world, adorned with God's strength and beauty, as a testimony of God's everlasting life.

Appendix

"But I lavish my love on those who love me and obey my
commands, even for a thousand generations"
(Exodus 20:6 NLT).

Scriptures to Pray for Grandchildren

(Insert your grandchild's name.)

Dear Father, I pray _____ will:

- Listen to constructive criticism and correction, and through it gain understanding (Proverbs 15:31, 32)
- Be quick to listen, slow to speak, and slow to become angry (James 1:19)
- Cast all his/her anxieties and disappointments on You to experience your care for him/her (1 Peter 5:7)
- Understand that the Lord is his/her helper and will always help him/her in every situation (Hebrews 13:6)
- Be kind, compassionate, and forgiving to others (Ephesians 4:32)
- Learn the secret of contentment in every situation (Philippians 4:12)
- Acknowledge You in all his/her ways and You will direct his/her path (Proverbs 3:6)
- Pursue righteousness, faith, love, and peace and enjoy the companionship of those who love the Lord (2 Timothy 2:22)
- Find a spouse with a growing relationship with Jesus Christ (2 Corinthians 6:14)
- Be generous and willing to share with others (1 Timothy 6:18)
- Be a good listener and think before he/she speaks (James 1:19)
- Guard his/her heart, for it is the wellspring of his/her life (Proverbs 4:23)
- Hunger and thirst for Your Word (Matthew 5:6)

- Do nothing out of selfish ambition, always thinking of others better than him/herself (Philippians 2:3)
- Show his/her love for You by his/her obedience to You (John 14:15)
- Learn to obey his/her parents (Ephesians 6:1)
- Not worry about anything, but pray about everything (Philippians 4:6)
- Be alert and watch out for the temptations from the enemy, standing firm in his/her faith (1 Peter 5:8, 9)
- Learn to be responsible for his/her own actions and behavior (Galatians 6:5)
- Believe that Jesus loves him/her and died for his/her sins so he/she can have a personal relationship with You and enjoy eternal life (John 3:16)
- Always remember that You will never leave nor forsake him/her (Joshua 1:5)
- Live in this evil world with self-control, right conduct, and devotion to God (Titus 2:12)
- Develop a servant's heart, serving wholeheartedly, as to the Lord and not men (Ephesians 6:7)
- Keep his/her tongue from evil and keep his/her lips from lying (Psalm 34:13)
- Be rooted and built up in his/her faith, growing strong in the truth (Colossians 2:7)
- Give You the desires of his/her heart and You will make his/her plans succeed (Psalm 20:4)
- Learn to give thanks in everything, no matter what happens (1 Thessalonians 5:18)
- Not have a spirit of fear and timidity, but the spirit of power, love, and self-discipline (2 Timothy 1:7)

- Trust You with all his/her heart and not depend on his/her own understanding (Proverbs 3:5)
- Will ask You when he/she needs wisdom (James 1:5)
- Work hard and cheerfully at all he/she does, pleasing the Lord, not men (Colossians 3:23)

By Lillian Penner

Note: There are thirty-one items in the list above. You may pray the same Scripture for each grandchild each day. On the other hand, on the first day of the month, pray the first item above for the oldest grandchild, then the next to the oldest, and down the line to the youngest. On the second day of the month, start with the next verse. This method will allow you to pray each scripture for each child individually during the month.

More Scriptures to Pray for Children and Grandchildren

Dear Father, I pray that (insert child's name)

1. Maturity in Faith
_____will grow in wisdom and stature and favor with God and man, just as Jesus did (Luke 2:52).

2. Encourager of Others
_____will be an encourager and build up the self-worth of others (1 Thessalonians 5:11).

3. Resist Temptation
You will give _____wisdom and strength to withstand temptation (1 Corinthians 10:13).

4. God's Word
_____will not merely listen to your Word but do what it says (James 1:22).

5. Protection
You will strengthen and protect _____from the evil one (2 Thessalonians 3:3).

6. Self-control
_____ will be self-controlled and alert, resisting the enemy and standing strong in their faith (1 Peter 5:8–9).

7. Compassionate
_____will become useful, helpful, kind, tenderhearted, and forgiving to others (Ephesians 4:32).

8. Anger
_____will rid him/herself from anger, hatred, cursing, and dirty language (Colossians 3:8).

9. Courage
_____will be strong and courageous, knowing God will be with them (Joshua 1:9).

10. Obedience

_____ will turn his/her eyes away from worthless things, living in obedience to your Word (Psalm 119:37).

11. Love for God's Word

_____will delight in your Word (Psalm 1:2).

12. Understand

You will show your strong love to _____ in ways he/she can understand (Psalm 17:7).

13. Trust

_____will trust in your unfailing love that surrounds him/her (Psalm 32:10).

14. Turn from Sin

_____will turn from all known sin and spend his/her time in doing good (Psalm 34:14).

15. Conversation/Words

_____will let his/her conversation be gracious, as well as sensible (Colossians 4:5).

16. Wise Choices

You will show _____how to distinguish right from wrong and how to make wise choices (Proverbs 2:9).

17. Not Misled

_____will not be misled, remembering that he/she can't ignore you and get away with it (Galatians 6:7).

18. Desire for God

_____will have a deep desire to seek you with his/her whole heart and not stray from the instructions in your Word (Psalm 119:10).

19. Sexual Purity

_____will live in this culture with its many temptations, flee from sexual immorality, and maintain purity for his/her future spouse (1 Corinthians 6:18).

20. Loving God

_____will have a passion for loving you with all his/her heart, soul, strength, and mind (Luke 10:27).

21. Live in Peace

_____will try to live in peace with everyone: work hard at it (Psalm 34:14).

22. Know Right from Wrong

_____will do what he/she knows is right, because knowing it and then not doing it is sin (James 4:17).

23. Controls Temper

_____will keep her/himself under control when angry, because a wise man holds his temper (Proverbs 29:11).

24. God-Directed Steps

_____will allow you to direct his/her steps because you delight in every detail of his/her life (Psalm 37:23).

25. Refuse Evil

_____will hate the gatherings of those who do evil and refuse to join in with the wicked (Psalm 26:5).

26. Satisfaction

_____will do his/her very best, for then he/she will have the personal satisfaction of work well done (Galatians 6:4).

27. Self-centeredness

_____will not just think about his/her own self but be interested in others and in what they are doing (Philippians 2:4).

29. Salvation

_____will believe that Jesus died on the cross for his/her sins, was buried, and rose from the dead so he/she could have a relationship with you (1 Corinthians 15:3–5).

Scriptures to Pray for Your Teen Grandchildren

Dear Father, I pray that (insert child's name)

SALVATION

_____will confess their sin and receive God's forgiveness and salvation found only through Christ (Acts 4:12).

PROTECTION FROM EVIL

_____will be protected from the evil one as they seek to live as followers of Christ (John 17:15).

DISCERNMENT

_____will be able to discern what is true and will have the courage to walk in the truth (Philippians 1:9–11).

IDENTITY

_____will understand they are uniquely designed, made in the image of God, male and female (Genesis 1:26–27).

BIBLICAL VIEW OF MARRIAGE

_____(and their future spouse) will have a biblical view of loving one another in marriage (Ephesians 5:22–23).

CHOICE OF FRIENDS

_____will choose friends who have integrity, sound judgment, and pure hearts (Psalm 1:1).

DEPRESSION (AND SUICIDAL TENDENCIES)

_____will be protected from the grip of depression, addiction, and suicidal tendencies (Luke 4:16–21).

SEXUAL IMMORALITY

_____will flee from sexual immorality in order to honor their bodies as the temple of the living God (1 Thessalonians 4:3–5).

RELATIONSHIP WITH PARENTS

_____will obey and respect their parents, for this is right (Ephesians 6:1–3).

HUNGER FOR THE WORD

_____will discover the transforming power of God's living and infallible Word (Hebrews 4:12).

CLOTHED IN RIGHTEOUSNESS

_____will be clothed in God's righteousness, justified by faith in Jesus (Romans 3:21–22).

RESISTING TEMPTATION

_____will be sober-minded and watching, resisting temptation by walking in the Spirit (Galatians 5:16–17).

TREATMENT OF OTHERS

_____will treat others with compassion, patience, forgiveness, and love (Colossians 3:13–14).

WISDOM IN MAKING DECISIONS

_____will possess wisdom and knowledge of God's will when facing difficult decisions (Colossians 1:9–10).

ENDURANCE

_____will be able to endure persecution and suffering when standing up for the truth (1 Peter 3:13–16).

ABIDE IN CHRIST

_____will abide in Christ and bear much fruit (John 15:5).

PRAYER

_____will have a powerful and effective prayer life (James 5:16).

DISCIPLINE AND SELF-CONTROL

_____will live in this evil world with self-control, right conduct, and devotion to God (Titus 2:1–12).

SERVANT'S HEART

_____will develop a servant's heart, doing nothing out of selfish ambition but serving God wholeheartedly (Mark 9:35).

FAITH

_____will be rooted and built up in faith (Colossians 2:7).

ACCEPT ADVICE

_____will listen to advice and accept instruction (Psalm 19:20).

TONGUE

_____will avoid calamity by guarding their mouth and tongue (Proverbs 21:23).

MANAGEMENT OF TIME, MONEY, AND TALENTS

_____will be prudent, seeking God's wisdom and direction in their management of time, money, and talents (Proverbs 3:5–6).

COMPARISONS

_____will not compare themselves with others but will find contentment in who they are, what they have, and how God has gifted them (Galatians 6:4).

RESPONSIBILITY

_____will learn to be responsible for their actions and behavior (Galatians 6:5).

GUARD HEART AND MIND

_____will guard their heart and mind with God's truth (Romans 12:2).

LOST SHEEP

_____will hear God's voice calling them when they have gone astray (Luke 15:11–32).

ACADEMICS

_____will be motivated and disciplined to apply themselves in the pursuit of knowledge, for God's glory and purposes (Colossians 3:23).

HUMILITY

_____will not do anything out of selfish ambition or conceit (Philippians 2:3–4).

THANKSGIVING

_____will learn to give thanks in everything, regardless of the circumstance (1 Thessalonians 5:18).

RELATIONSHIP WITH CHRIST

_____will live the adventure of following Jesus Christ as Lord by loving as Christ has loved them (John 15:12, 15–17).

By Lillian Penner and Sherry Schumann

Scriptures for Grandparents to Pray for Themselves

Lord, I pray for . . .

THE SPIRIT OF WISDOM

Give me your spirit of wisdom and insight to know you better (Ephesians 1:17).

MY ROLE AS A GRANDPARENT

Help me teach your Word and share my faith with my grandchildren (Deuteronomy 4:9).

STEADFASTNESS

Help me stand firm and resist the devil's schemes by putting on the armor of God (Ephesians 6:11).

FAITH

Help me to remain rooted and built up in biblical faith (Colossians 2:6–7).

NONCONFORMITY

Help me let the things of this world diminish and my love for you increase (Romans 12:2).

EXAMPLE OF GODLY LIVING

Help me show my grandchildren what a godly life looks like in a secular world (Titus 2:7–8).

WISE USE OF TIME

Help me make the most of the opportunities I have and not foolishly waste them (Ephesians 5:15–17).

AWARENESS OF HYPOCRISY

Show me when my actions don't match my words (James 1:22–25).

FAITHFULNESS IN MY MARRIAGE

Help me model a godly marriage for my family (Ephesians 5:22, 25).

A HUNGER FOR GOD'S WORD

Help me spend time reading and pondering the truth of your Word (2 Timothy 3:16–17).

A BIBLICAL WORLDVIEW

Help me develop a biblical world view by placing my hope in Christ during this time of uncertainty and ungodliness (Hebrews 6:19).

A SAFE HAVEN

Help me provide a secure environment where my grandchildren will feel safe to ask questions and share their struggles and disappointments (Ephesians 4:29; James 1:19).

FORGIVENESS

Help me apologize when my words or actions hurt my family and forgive them when they hurt me (Matthew 5:23–24).

HEALTHY RELATIONSHIPS

Help me relate and connect to my grandchildren with wisdom and love, even when it's awkward (Isaiah 44:3).

MY MIND

Help me guard what enters my mind and resist the enemy by focusing on you (Philippians 4:8).

OBEDIENCE TO CHRIST

Help me remain in Christ and obey his commands (John 15:10–15).

DISCERNMENT

Direct my prayers by giving me discernment about the vulnerable spots and unguarded doors of my grandchildren's hearts (Proverbs 4:23).

BLESSINGS FOR MY GRANDCHILDREN

Provide opportunities for me to teach them that they are your workmanship and you have a plan for their lives (Ephesians 2:10).

WORSHIP

Help me to offer praise to God, even in difficult circumstances (Hebrews 13:15).

HONOR

As a parent, show me how to honor my parents; as a grandparent, show me how to honor my adult children (Romans 12:19).

FERVENCY IN PRAYER

Keep me on my knees in all things (Ephesians 6:18).

LISTENING SKILLS

Teach me to be a good listener who responds to my grand-children without anger or harsh criticism (James 1:19).

INTENTIONAL DISCIPLESHIP

Make me a disciple who encourages my grandchildren to a mature faith in Jesus Christ (Philippians 1:9–11; Colossians 4:12).

A REPENTANT HEART

Make my life an example of true repentance when I stray from your truth (Revelation 2:2–5).

SELF-DENIAL

Give me the fortitude to deny myself and follow Christ (Mark 8:34).

FRUIT OF THE SPIRIT

Let your Holy Spirit fall afresh on me so I may bear abundant fruit for a hungry world (Galatians 5:22–23).

WISDOM OF THE HOLY SPIRIT

Grant me wisdom in all circumstances (James 1:5).

RESISTANCE TO TEMPTATION

Help me to be sober-minded and watching, resisting temptation by walking in the Spirit (Galatians 5:16–17).

HOPE

Fill me with hope and joy to the point of overflowing to my family (Romans 15:13).

MY MOUTH

Help me avoid calamity by guarding my mouth and tongue (Proverbs 21:23).

By Lillian Penner and Sherry Schumann

Lillian Ann Penner

Photo Prayer Journal for My Grandchildren

(Place a picture of your grandchild here)

"Devote yourself to prayer, being watchful and thankful"
(Colossians 4:2).

Photo Prayer Journal

A photo prayer journal is a working document to help grandparents pray effectively for their grandchildren, whether they live far away or nearby. The photo prayer journal will make praying more meaningful. You will feel more of a connection when you see the pictures of your grandchildren as you are praying for them. Make your own photo prayer journal using the example in this section in a three ring binder. Then you can redo it each year when your grandchildren start a new school year.

Instructions for Photo Prayer Journal Profile Sheet

On the profile sheet, place your grandchild's picture in the designated spot and complete the profile with his/her information.

Instructions for Prayer Concern Sheet

Record the date, praises, prayer concerns, and the hopes and dreams for your grandchild on which you want to focus your prayers. If desired, choose a scripture from the "Scriptures to Pray for Grandchildren" or the list of "Prayer Suggestions for the Various Life's Stages" or other suggestions from this book. Write down concerns about their safety and health, physical, mental, emotional, and spiritual growth, strength to resist temptations, etc.

Suggestions

I do not use the photo prayer journal every day, only once or twice a week. However, it does help me to connect with the grandchildren more often, especially in my thoughts.

If convenient, take your grandchildren out for a meal or ice cream to ask them for the information needed to fill out the profile sheets, and tell them why you are doing it. You may also ask them the questions on the telephone, through e-mail, or however you find it most convenient.

If you are making the journal on the computer, use Print Shop or another program to enhance the pages, inserting your digital pictures, and making as many pages as you need.

Sample Profile Sheet

(Place your grandchild's picture here.)

Profile Sheet for Grandchild

Year: <u>2010</u>

Name: Carol Brown
Address: 12345 First St., Midtown, Any state Telephone : (621) 123-4567 Cell #
E-mail address: carolb@yahoo.com Birthday: April 1, 1995 Age: 11 years
Grade in school: 5th School: Lincoln Elementary Teacher: Mrs. Scott
Church: Southwest Hills Baptist Church Friends: Alice, Susie, Nancy and Mary
Favorite activities: soccer, softball, ballet, swimming, piano, camping
Character strengths: performing, reading, good student, organization

Grandchild's Profile

(Place your grandchild's picture here.)

Profile Sheet For _____ **Date** _____

Name:
Address:
Telephone # Home   Cell #
E-mail address:
Birthday:
          Age:
Grade in school:
Name of School:
Teacher:
Church:
Friends:
Favorite activities:
Character strengths:

Prayer Focus For _____

Date: **Praises:**

_____

_____

_____

_____

_____

_____

_____

Date: **Requests:**

_____

_____

_____

_____

_____

_____

_____

_____

_____

_____

_____

_____

_____

_____

_____

_____

_____

_____

Your Grandchild's Favorites

Name _____

Color _____
Animal _____
Ice cream flavor _____
Fruit _____
Vegetable _____
Dessert _____
Fast food restaurant _____
Pizza _____
Beverage _____
Soft drink _____
Toy _____
Spectator sport _____
Sport involvement _____
Movie _____
Vacation _____
Friends _____
TV program _____
Book _____
Song _____
Subject in school _____

Introducing Grandparents@Prayer

"The prayer of a righteous man (grandparent) is powerful and effective" (James 5:16c).

We are living in challenging times morally and spiritually, especially for our grandchildren. A media-driven culture has desensitized our grandchildren and pushed the boundaries of a Christ-like lifestyle. "The role of grandparenting is becoming more important than anyone would ever have imagined. The rescue of our culture may well rest on the shoulders of today's grandparents. What an incredible call for the second half of life."[1] Do we, as grandparents, understand the mighty and powerful force that prayer can be for our grandchildren in these times?

Years ago, Esther stood in the gap with prayer for her people, the Israelites, when their lives were threatened. Today grandparents can stand in the gap with prayer for their grandchildren just as Esther stood in the gap for her people.

As grandparents, we can make a significant difference in the world by praying regularly and deliberately for our grandchildren and their parents. We have an opportunity to powerfully touch the lives of another generation for eternity.

Christian Grandparenting Network has formed "Grandparents@ Prayer," intercessory prayer groups for grandparents to pray together for each other's grandchildren and families.

Here is the challenge I am laying before you. Will you take up the call to start a "Grandparents@Prayer" group in your area? Invite other grandparents in your area to join you to form a group to intercede for the next generations.

My husband and I participate in a Grandparents@ Prayer group and find it a blessing to unite in prayer with other grandparents for each other's grandchildren.

Format for starting a "Grandparents@Prayer" (G@P) group in your area:

Purpose: To call grandparents around the world to intentionally and regularly come together to pray and intercede for their grandchildren, children, and communities.

Goal: To encourage and provide resources for grandparents to be intentional prayer warriors for their grandchildren through the personal discipline of intercessory prayer in the battle against the enemy.

Structure: G@P consists of small or large groups of people meeting once or twice a month at a designated location for an hour for guided prayer and fellowship.

The greatest gift you can give your grandchildren is a praying grandparent.

> *"I have no greater joy than to hear that my children (grandchildren) are walking with the Lord"*
> (3 John 1:4).

If you would like to be a part of the G@P prayer ministry or start a group, contact:
Christian Grandparenting Network
www.christiangrandparenting.net/prayer

Grandparents@Prayer (G@P) Testimonials

A Grandmother in Oregon Shares:

I love the sweet fellowship, support, and friendships of my Grandparents @ Prayer Group. I feel safe to share my heavy heart for my grandchildren and their parents, knowing others will be praying for them too. It is wonderful to see how God is answering our prayers in the lives of our families as we pray for them.

A Grandmother in South Dakota Shares:

At our second Grandparents@Prayer meeting we had a new grandfather who came to pray for his grandson who is an army helicopter pilot in Iraq. He was concerned for the safety of his grandson and for his other grandchildren who are living all over the world. Tonight at Church the pastor asked him to share about attending the Grandparents@prayer meeting and praying for his grandson. On Wednesday he and his wife had already received an e-mail telling them that he was home and safe. He was so appreciative of all our prayers.

When I shared my Pastor he said, "There is something about prayers in a group vs.. only your own prayers. I can't tell you how excited I was to hear the excitement in their voices and them talking about their grandchildren and children.

A grandmother in Minnesota Shares:

Three G@P groups from our church have been gathering for prayer once or twice a month for almost ten years! It has been such a blessing for our families to know they are covered with corporate prayer. God answered our prayers when our group prayed for our four-year-old granddaughter last summer as she was suffering from a rare illness and hospitalized for several days. God answered our prayers, and she was healed. It is comforting to know that others care for my family and pray for my family's needs when I share my concerns with them. We pray blessings for our families, as well. We all share our prayer requests for our families as we meet monthly and ask for prayer and praises via e-mail at any time.

Our precious Lord deeply yearns for our prayers and desires us to petition his blessings upon our families. The Holy Spirit is so evident in this commitment to prayer! I challenge you to become a fervent praying parent or grandparent so that you may become God's blessing to the generations that follow you!

Introducing Grandparents' Day of Prayer

The Power of United Prayer

It is a global reality that truth is under attack like never before in our schools, our political arenas, the market-place, and even in our churches. Christianity is under assault, and parents and grandparents find themselves involved in a tug-of-war for the hearts and minds of their children. It is not easy for our grandchildren to navigate in this post-Christian culture. Satan is relent-less in his aggressive attack to desensitize our children to truth and righteousness.

This is a spiritual battle requiring spiritual weap-ons. Our grandchildren and their parents not only need our support, they need our earnest prayers. **They need our united prayer, a genuine, unified prayer for our hope and dreams for the next generation to be realized.** Jesus declared, "Again I say to you that if two believers on earth agree [that is, are of one mind, in harmony] about anything that they ask [within the will of God], it will be done for them by my Father in heaven. For where two or three are gathered in my name [meeting together as my followers], I am there among them" (Matt. 18:19–20).

Christian Grandparenting Network (CGN) is claiming National Grandparents' Day on the second Sunday in September as a Grandparents' Day of Prayer. **We believe the battle for the hearts and minds of our dear grandchildren** and their parents can be won only by praying grandparents who sense the urgency and unite to do battle in prayer.

In the past, united prayer has always bridged the gap between a great need and a great awakening! **Our grandchildren and their parents urgently need our unified prayers.** Let's be a community of grandparents uniting in prayer for our families.

CGN would like to invite all praying grandparents to join us to come before God's throne of grace to obtain mercy and find grace in our time of need for our grandchildren and their parents.

More information is available on the website: https://christiangrandparenting.net/grandparents-day-of-prayer/

Will you join us for the next Grandparents' Day of Prayer?

Testimonials of Grandparents' Day of Prayer

A grandparent in Missouri writes. We had a great time of Prayer and reading the scriptures on Sunday. We had around 70 in attendance. We started with a box lunch then kind of followed the outline in the Resource booklet you provided. We had two testimonies of grandmas praying for their grands and how God answered prayer. Then the pastor led us in a guided prayer time. We finished up by everyone reading the Grandparents Declaration then the Steve Green video of "Find us Faithful." It was a good time of prayer and fellowship. I have heard great comments about it and people wanting to do it again next year. Thank you for providing all the great resources.

A grandparent in Oregon writes . . .We started our evening with a little reflection and sharing about what we had learned from our own grandparents. Great nuggets were shared that inspire us onward in our journey and then a time of prayer. We have been meeting once a month for a year and our attendance has remained between 10 and 15. We are growing closer and feeling a greater sense of support.

A grandparent in South Dakota writes . . .With a team of six people we hosted a prayer event in our basement...nine additional precious grandparents came.. Such a sweet presence of the Holy Spirit. As we asked people why they had come, two desires were spoken repeatedly...looking for deeper relationships with God and others, and hungry for tools and ideas to grow in prayer for their grandchildren, and relationally with their grandchildren. Precious sharing/prayer at small group tables. We were so grateful, humbled as God knit our hearts in prayer, creating a safe place for people to open up and pour out their hearts. We closed singing together "May all who come behind us find us faithful", using a U-tube with the words and melody... and then joined in a circle in prayer together.

A grandparent in Queensland, Australia writes . . .My church on the Sunshine Coast in Queensland Australia had 35 grandparents join in prayer on September 23 for our Grandparents Day of Prayer. I shared with them about my praying auntie who supported me with prayer throughout my life. She recently went to be with the Lord aged 92. The morning was very successful and all enjoyed morning tea afterwards. Future events are being planned.

A Grandparent in Oregon writes . . .I believe giving grandparents a scriptural format to use when they pray for their grandchildren are invaluable; plus the encouragement to ask our grandchildren how we can pray for them. The guest speaker was living proof of the faith her grandparents shared with her. The stories she told about the blessings of having had grandparents who prayed for her was inspirational to me. Those stories and examples were concrete tools given to the guests.

About Christian Grandparenting Network

Christian Grandparenting Network (CGN) is a Christian organization devoted to challenging those in mid-life and beyond to finish the race well by living for future generations. CGN is committed to helping individuals and churches cultivate "intentionality" in an inter-generational ministry by focusing on and strengthening the grandparent-grandchild relationship. We live in a time when the darkness of sin and unrighteousness is sweeping over our land with ferocity seeking to engulf the minds and hearts of our youth and young families.

We are in a battle for the minds and hearts of each of the emerging generations of our time because there is a problem with the "light" today. Grandparents are front line warriors in that spiritual battle!

We are in desperate need of older generations who will step to the plate and hold out the light of God's Word and the Gospel of Jesus Christ. Unfortunately, a large segment of our older generation has given in to the modern notion of retirement, resulting in the greatest waste of human resources in the entire history of mankind. The light has been dimmed, if not completely hidden, for our next generations.

Dietrich Bonheoffer declared more than sixty years ago that "a righteous man lives for the next generation." At CGN, we believe that is also a biblical mandate from God.

The Church is the last place in our society where all of the generations still gather in one place at least one day a week. Sadly, little opportunity is seized to utilize this "family" gathering to connect the generations in meaningful and life-changing relationships as God intended.

There is a huge need for belonging and connecting among every generation. Yet, because we are so disconnected and compartmentalized even in our churches, each generation has developed its own culture, which exacerbates the disconnection from a sense of belonging to a larger, vital family. The grandparenting role is one that can reverse this trend and build strong, healthy families united in God's love. Check out the Christian Grandparenting Network website to read valuable grandparenting helps each week on www. christiangrandparenting.com.

Mission Statement

The Mission of Christian Grandparenting Network is to promote effective grandparenting, which is intentionally about helping our children and grandchildren know and follow Christ anywhere wholeheartedly.

Vision

Our vision is to be a vehicle for networking and to provide a variety of resources to aid people who are involved with grandparenting. We also seek to provide purposeful, powerful opportunities for inter-generational dialogue, strengthening family relationships, evangelism, and personal spiritual growth.

Suggested Reading for Praying Grandparents

Pass the Legacy:
7 Keys for Grandparents Making a Difference
Catherine Jacobs
Nashville, TN: Elm Hill, 2018

Courageous Grandparenting:
Building a Legacy Worth Outliving You
Cavin Harper
Christian Grandparenting Network

GrandParenting:
Strengthening Your Family and Passing on Your Faith
Dr. Josh Mulvihill
Bloomington, MN: Bethany House Publishers, 2018

Legacy of Prayer:
A Spiritual Trust Fund for the Generations
Jennifer Kennedy Dean
Birmingham, AL: New Hope Publishers, 2002

Overcoming Grandparenting Barriers
How to Navigate Painful Problems with Grace and Truth
Larry Fowler
Bloomington, MN: Bethany House Publishers, 2019

The H.E.A.R.T
5 Keys to Being the Best Grandparent Possible
Ken R. Canfield, PhD
Siloam Springs, AR: DaySpring, 2018

A Practical Guide to Culture
Helping the Next Generation Navigate Today's World
John Stonestreet & Brett Kunkle
Colorado Springs, CO: David C. Cook, 2017

Praying with Purpose
Taking Your Prayer Life from Vague to Victorious
Deborah Haddix
Anderson, IN: Warner Press, 2018

Soul Nourishment:
Satisfying Our Deep Longing for God
Deborah Haddix
Anderson, IN: Warner Press, 2018

Footnotes

God uses People to Bridge the Gap

1. Jennifer Kennedy Dean, Live a Praying Life, (Birmingham, AL: New Hope Publishers, 2003). p 60.

Communicating Your Faith

1. Helen Kooiman Hosier, Living the Lois Legacy, (Wheaton, IL, Tyndale House, 2002), p. 66.

2. Believing God Bible study, Beth Moore, Life-Way Press, 2002

3. Jennifer Kennedy Dean, Legacy of Prayer, Birmingham, New Hope Publishers, p. 15.

4. Ibid p 48–49

A Look at your Grandchild's Culture

1. John Stonestreet & Brett Kunkle, A Practical Guide to   Culture, David C. Cook Publisher, 2017, p 153–155.

God's Gift of Intercessory Prayer

1. "Soldiers' Children Struggle, Too," Parade Magazine, December 20, 2009, p 6.

2. Used by permission from Peggy Powell, Praying Grandmother's Newsletter. Fall-Winter 2009–2010.

Praying God's Word

1. Jennifer Kennedy Dean, Live a Praying Life, (Birmingham: New Hope Publishers, 2003), p. 31

2. Used by permission from Praying Grandmothers, newsletter by Peggy Powell, Fall 2009.

Making Wise Choices

1. Quin Sherrer & Ruthanne Garlock, Grandma, I Need Your Prayers, (Grand Rapids, MI: Zondervan, 2002), p. 165–166.

Choosing Friends Wisely

1. Used by permission from Peggy Powell, Praying Grandmothers fall 2009 Newsletter and Sandy Edmonson, 2010.

Connecting with Grandchildren

1. Helen Kooiman Hosier, Living the Lois Legacy (Wheaton, IL: Tyndale House Publishers, 2002), p. 109. A Focus on the Family Book.

Introducing "Grandparents@Prayer (G@P

1. Randy Swanson, Broken magazine, issue May/June 2009,

About the Author

Lillian Ann Penner is an author, blogger, speaker, and grandmother residing with her husband, John, in Portland, Oregon. They have been married for more than fifty years and have three married sons, nine grandchildren, and five great-grandchildren.

Penner is the Co-Prayer Director for Christian Grandparenting Network., She provides resources and writes about her passion for grandparents to pray intentionally for their grandchildren and their parents. She also blogs twice weekly on her website "Grandparenting with a Purpose." She is the founder of Grandparents@Prayer intercessory prayer groups and Grandparents' Day of Prayer. She facilitates two Grandparents@Prayer groups.

Lillian has been active in church ministry for over fifty years, leading an outreach ministry for young mothers, a mentoring ministry for women, and various other church ministries. She has participated in short-term missions in the Ukraine and has volunteered with several Christian ministries.

She and her husband enjoy traveling and listening to Southern Gospel music, but most of all they love spending time with their children, grandchildren, and great-grandchildren.

Order Information

REDEMPTION
PRESS

To order additional copies of this book, please visit:

www.redemption-press.com

Also available on www.redemption-press.com
Or by calling toll free 1-844-2REDEEM

CPSIA information can be obtained
at www.ICGtesting.com
Printed in the USA
BVHW071736131119
563721BV00002B/268/P

9 781632 325730